THE SHAKING & AWAKENING

GIFT SEASON EIGHT

THOMAS A PETTERSON

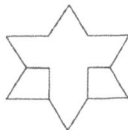

COPYRIGHT

The Shaking & Awakening

Season Eight

© 2025 Thomas A. Petterson

Publishing Details:

Paperback ISBN: 978-1-7642449-0-9

eBook ISBN ePub: 978-1-76424449-1-6

eBook ISBN Kindle 978-1-7642449-2-3

Ebook Version GIFT Seasons 1-8:

Season 1-7 1st Edition 2014, ePub and Mobi

Season 1-8 2nd Edition 2015, ePub and Mobi

Season 1-8 RePublished March 2023, ePub and Mobi

ISBN:9781925029895

Troubled Waters Dead Ahead Season 9:

ISBN 979-8-231-09552-0

Book Cover Design: BookCovers.com

✿ Formatted with Vellum

CONTENTS

DEDICATION

Holy, holy, holy is the Lord God Almighty.
Blessing, glory, wisdom, thanksgiving, honour, power and
might, be to our God and the Lamb who sits at His Right Hand.
All honour to Ruach HaKodesh, the Spirit of Truth who guides us
into all truth, who speaks not on His own initiative but says only
what he hears.
With special thanks to Julie-Ann my ever patient editor, team
mate and love of my life.

INTRODUCTION

I have found that Abba Father *(Yahweh)* always tells me what I need to know ahead of time or when I need to know it. The words in The Shaking and Awakening are mainly from Season Eight ebook which were previously published in 2015. They were relevant then but now ten years on the insights and instructions are more urgent as the state of the world is daily deteriorating and the harbingers prophesied by Yeshua *(Jesus)* are upon us. *Matthew 24:6-8 "You will hear of wars and rumours of wars. See that you aren't troubled, for all this must happen, but the end is not yet. For nation will rise against nation, and kingdom against kingdom; and there will be famines, plagues, and earthquakes in various places. But all these things are the beginning of birth pains. WEB.*

Connecting with Ruach HaKodesh *(Holy Spirit)* is so simple that most miss it. Begin by stopping whatever you have been doing and learn to sit in His presence. As simple as breathing in and breathing out!

If we allow Yahweh and Yeshua to love us we will expe-rience a Niagara Falls type encounter as their great Love washes over us, enriching, refreshing and renewing us each and every day-FOREVER!

I trust the words of Season Eight will be instructive and inspirational and help you to not only survive but thrive in the coming days of The Shaking and Awakening.

Thomas A Petterson
Prophetic Scribe

Contact Details:
    Email: giftbook@pm.me
    Website: www.giftbook.net
    Facebook: facebook.com/godlyinsightsfortoday

GIFT-Godly Insights For Today:
    Ebook Seasons 1-8
    Troubled Waters Dead Ahead Season Nine
    The Shaking & Awakening Season Eight
    Paperback and eBook.
    https://giftbook.net/buy-now/

BIBLE QUOTATIONS

GLOSSARY

The following names and titles are used throughout this book.

Yeshua : Jesus.

Yeshua HaMashiach : Jesus theMessiah

Abba : An affectionate way to say "father".

Ruach HaKodesh : Holy Spirit.

Yahweh : God.

Yahweh Sabaoth : Lord of Hosts.

Adonai : Lord.

Adonai Eloheinu : Lord God.

Adonai Echad : Lord is One. Mark 12:29.

Elyon : God Most High.

Shaddai : God Almighty.

Elohim : Supreme Mighty One;
The God Of Israel.

Ehyeh-Asher-Ehyeh : I am Who I Am;
I will Be What I Will Be.

Echad : One. Numerical Number 13.

Sh'ma : Hear oh Israel.

Malki-Tzedek : Melchizedek. Priest of the Most

High God.

Mashiach Ben-Ha M'vorakh : The messiah, Son of the Blessed One.

HaG'vurah : The Power.

Tanakh : Old Testament.

Brit Hadashah : New Testament.

Torah : First Five Books of the Hebrew Bible.

Cohen Hagadol : High Priest.

Cohen : Priest.

Acharit Hyamim : The Last Days.

Rosh Hashanah : Jewish New Year.

Shavuot : Feast of Weeks - Pentecost.

Shalom : Peace.

Yerushalayim : Jerusalem.

Y'hudah : Judea.

Shaul : Paul.

Moshe : Moses.

Kefa : Peter.

Goyim : Non-Jews.

Olam Hazeh : This Present World.

Talmidim : Disciples.

Mitzvot : Commandments; Obligation.

Eternity Past to Eternity Future : Everlasting to everlasting. *Psalm 41:14 (13) Blessed be Adonai the God of Isra'el from eternity past to eternity future. Amen. Amen. CJB.*

Paramours : paramours noun paramour (plural paramours) an illicit lover, either male or female.

Caveat : to qualify a particular statement with a proviso.

Calamity : an event causing great and often sudden damage or distress; a disaster.

Fortitude : strength of mind that enables a person

to encounter danger or bear pain or adversity
with courage.

Tribulation : an experience that tests one's endurance,
patience or faith.

Constancy : steadfastness, as in purpose or affection;
faithfulness. The condition or quality of being
constant; changelessness.

Panacea : remedy for all ills or difficulties; cure all.

Retribution : recompense, reward. The dispensing or
receiving of reward or punishment especially
in the hereafter.

Advocate : to speak for, support, or represent.

Daysman : an adjudicator, judge or intermediary.

Paraclete : mediator or advocate.

Chuppah : Huppah. Wedding canopy used in
Jewish weddings.

Shadow Lands : A shadowy or borderline area
where normal rules or boundaries do not apply.

Bush Fire : Australian term for wildfire.

FOREWORD

The shofars are sounding! Let all who have ears to hear, heed the sound of the heavenly shofars calling all of Yahweh's people everywhere, to prepare for what is soon to befall the world.

The body of Messiah has become complacent and needs to heed the ancient warning of the Jewish sages to wake up from our slumber and realise that the enemy has infiltrated the camp. There are many walking wounded some injured by friendly fire! Whatever happened to our understanding that we are at war with the dark kingdom?

"Onward Christian soldiers, marching as to war, with the cross of Jesus going on before! Christ, the royal Master leads against the foe, Forward into battle see His banner go!" Was written in 1865 (Baring – Gould). Have we forgotten we are at war or just gone to sleep?

"Arise from your slumber, you who are asleep, wake up from your deep sleep, you who are fast asleep; search your deeds, repent, and remember, your creator." (Maimonides)

I trust that the words in this book will be a wake up call for us all.

Correction and discipline are not concepts we are used to; but Abba Father disciplines and instructs those He loves.

Hebrews 12:6 *"For the Lord corrects and disciplines everyone whom He loves, and He punishes, even scourges, every son whom He accepts and welcomes to His heart and cherishes"* AMPC.

Deuteronomy 8:5-6 *"You shall consider in your heart that as a man disciplines his son, so Yahweh your God disciplines you. You shall keep the commandments of Yahweh your God, to walk in his ways, and to fear him."* WEB.

I have always known and related to the Son of God as Jesus. At age 16 I invited Him into my heart and acknowledged Jesus Christ as my Lord and Saviour. I love the name Jesus and all the songs that praise His name and all that it represents in my life and indeed are still in my spirit. However, since first visiting Israel in 1989 and discovering the Hebrew Roots of Christianity, I now find myself more comfortable using the names Yahweh *(God)*, Yeshua *(Jesus)* and Ruach HaKodesh *(Holy Spirit)*.

This is a personal choice and I find using these names helpful in moving towards the One New Man spoken of in Ephesians 2:19-22:

So then, you are no longer foreigners and strangers. On the contrary, you are fellow-citizens with God's people and members of God's family. You have been built on the foundation of the emissaries and the prophets, with the cornerstone being Yeshua the Messiah himself.

In union with him the whole building is held together, and it is growing into a holy temple in union with the Lord. Yes, in union with him, you yourselves are being built together into a spiritual dwelling-place for God! CJB.

The GIFT words that I receive from Holy Spirit *(Ruach HaKodesh)* are in the first person. Sometimes Jesus *(Yeshua)* is speaking, sometimes it is Holy Spirit *(Ruach*

HaKodesh) Himself and sometimes it is Abba Father *(Yahweh)*.

It took me a while to figure out who was talking as Holy Spirit *(Ruach HaKodesh)* relays to my spirit what He is hearing both Yeshua *(Jesus)* and Yahweh *(God)* saying, as well as His own words. Often it is not clear until the word is complete who is speaking, but on reflection it will present itself.

You will notice that there is no tense in the words, which is only logical as Heaven, Yeshua *(Jesus)* the Messiah, Yahweh *(God)* our Father the Great "I AM" and Ruach HaKodesh the Holy Spirit dwell outside of time.

Exodus 3:14-15 God said to Moshe, "Ehyeh Asher Ehyeh [I am/will be what I am/will be]," and added, "Here is what to say to the people of Isra'el: 'Ehyeh [I Am or I Will Be] has sent me to you.'"

God said further to Moshe, "Say this to the people of Isra'el: 'Yud-Heh-Vav-Heh [Adonai], the God of your fathers, the God of Avraham, the God of Yitz'chak and the God of Ya'akov, has sent me to you.' This is my name forever; this is how I am to be remembered generation after generation. CJB.

I trust that the insights and instructions in The Shaking and Awakening will challenge you as they have me and help us all to re-evaluate and revive our lives in Yeshua *(Jesus)*. I trust they will help us all to repair and prepare ourselves spiritually, giving us the courage and boldness to rise up against the evil one and his plans that confront us each and every day.

May we all remain faithful to Him who has called us until He comes. Yeshua *(Jesus)* told His disciples *"I have said these things to you so that, united with me, you may have shalom. In the world, you have tsuris. But be brave! I have conquered the world!" John 16:33 CJB.*

Hebrews 13:20-21 The God of shalom brought up from the dead the great Shepherd of the sheep, our Lord Yeshua, by the blood of an eternal covenant. May that God equip you with every good thing you need to do his will; and may he do in us whatever pleases him, through Yeshua the Messiah. To him be the glory forever and ever. Amen. CJB.

Thomas A. Petterson
Prophetic Scribe

CHAPTER 1

THE SHAKING & AWAKENING

ecember 8th 2008; 11th Kislev 5769.

The Time Has Come for a shaking of the Body of Yeshua. She is slumbering in complacency and ignorance of the time and the hour in which she lives. She has been bewitched by the gods of this world and has surrounded herself with paramours both wittingly and unwittingly. She will soon be shaken and the scales will begin to fall from her eyes; she will understand that the garden of delight she dwells in is not of My making. As My dawning light opens her eyes to see she will understand that her current comfortable garden of delight is an illusion; she will see that her true love is not to be found in this garden.

Her delight will immediately turn to despair because she will realise she has been duped; now a great chasm separates her from her true garden of delight. She can now plainly see that the garden she is in is precariously poised on the edge of a vast precipice that was designed to crumble and collapse into the dark abyss of hopelessness and despair.

She will awaken as I gently shake her and see that the true path to the true garden of delight where she can wait in safety for My appearance is on the other side of this vast chasm. The shaking will be gentle at first. As the earth rumbles and shakes the very foundation of the garden she found herself in will crumble beneath her feet and unless she runs for her life she will be swallowed up by Satan's wicked plans.

There is a mountain she must flee to for her safety and it is clear and plain for her to find. The only path to safety is over My mountain with all of its rocks and crags and difficult passages which lead to the other side of the vast chasm that is even now opening up wider and wider. I'm calling to her firstly from My mountain; for it is here that I can protect her. It is here on the mountain of the Lord that she will meet with her maker and creator who will provide for her supernaturally through the difficult tribulations that are even now beginning throughout the earth.

Isaiah 2:2-3 It shall happen in the latter days, that the mountain of Yahweh's house shall be established on the top of the mountains, and shall be raised above the hills; and all nations shall flow to it.

Many peoples shall go and say, "Come, let's go up to the mountain of Yahweh, to the house of the God of Jacob; and he will teach us of his ways, and we will walk in his paths." For out of Zion the law shall go out, and Yahweh's word from Jerusalem. WEB.

As she comes to Me with a pure and penitent heart I will draw her unto Myself and guide her in paths of safety; into the good pastures and My true garden of delight. There she will be made ready to be swept into My arms when the time of betrothal is ended. My bride to be needs to come back to My mountain and be purified and again set on fire with a fresh love for Me and be transformed into My radiant bride; ready to be swept into My arms when the time of betrothal is ended. *Revelation 19:8 It was given to her that she would array herself in bright, pure, fine linen, for the fine linen is the righteous acts of the saints. WEB.*

Surrounded by the multitudes of heaven the marriage ceremony will take place under the Royal Chuppah and lead on to the prophesied Marriage Supper of The Lamb.

Revelation 19:6b-7 Hallelujah! For the Lord our God, the Almighty, reigns! Let's rejoice and be exceedingly glad, and let's give the glory to Him. For the wedding of the Lamb has come, and his wife has made herself ready. WEB.

Sadly many will not leave the garden of deception; putting faith in past experiences and their own foolish pride which led them to this place. And even as the ground opens up beneath their feet they will still hold onto their strong beliefs; refusing to heed the warnings of the prophets and even My voice calling to them from My mountain.

The Shaking & Awakening was first published in GIFT Godly Insights For Today Season Six ebook 2014.

CHAPTER 2
NEW SHOES

Yom Kippur 10th Tishrei 5775; October 4th 2014.

Yahweh Speaks: New Shoes speak of many things. It is symbolic of a new day or a new direction or a new commission. Shoes are foundational for any dress code. If you are hiking you will need shoes that are suitable for rough terrain that will protect your feet from damage; shoes that will give you a sure footing in dangerous rocky climbs or stability on slippery surfaces. Polished leather dress shoes are important for official occasions and the shoes themselves indicate the type of activity that is about to be undertaken. Uniforms always include appropriate well-made shoes that are suitable for the duties that will be encountered.

The issue of New Shoes indicates a change is taking place and the attire you used to wear is no longer suitable or appropriate for the office or duties that are about to be undertaken. The shoes that I issue speak of the Gospel of Peace and the shoes that I issued to My disciples were to spread the Gospel; each set of shoes taking them on the individual journey that was planned for them ahead of time. Their spiritual shoes were tailor-made for the tasks and commissions I sent them on and in their days on the earth they served them well.

Today I am issuing you with New Shoes that represent the new season in your life that will enable you to fulfil My commission for you and your family. New Shoes speak of an end to your journey thus far; the old shoes that have served you well and taken you to many familiar places are being replaced with the new that will lead you to different destinations of My choosing. It is not necessarily that the old shoes are worn out; it is that they have served their purpose and will not be suitable for the days that lie ahead. Old shoes are comfortable and there is the familiarity of doing things the same way day in and day out that they represent.

New Shoes can be uncomfortable for a while until you break them in; quite often you will put the old shoes back on but there comes the realisation that it is time to move on, put on the New Shoes and get used to them. Your New Shoes will help you stand tall and correct your posture and bring you back into line with My will and purposes for your life. There are new garments that come with the New Shoes; garments of praise and joy, bright and cheery, again of My choosing. Strip off the garment of heaviness and death; leave behind the house of horror and My New Shoes will direct your paths from this very day.

Your New Shoes speak of hope. They represent a new beginning, a new day, open heavens and a release from the past. They speak of adventure, friends, health, prosperity, fulfilment, meaning and purpose. These have been lacking in your life due to many pressures but I am directing your paths from now on and the future is looking brighter for you and all who are serving Me with full hearts in these dark days.

I am not issuing you with your full uniform or spiritual attire for the future; for now I am giving you your New Shoes as I want you to wear them and break them in. Sufficient for you to know that I am directing your steps and the New Shoes speak of new direction, new beginnings, and the new office assigned to you by Ruach HaKodesh and a sure foundation of hope for your future.

As you walk out your destiny one step at a time be assured that the New Shoes will take you where I direct you and will bring you to divine appointments on time and right in season. Moses was issued with New Shoes at the burning bush. I told him to take off his old shoes because the ground he was standing on was holy ground. After his encounter with Me he was commissioned and he left that place wearing his New Shoes.

Exodus 3:1-5 Now Moses was keeping the flock of Jethro, his father-in-law, the priest of Midian, and he led the flock to the back of the wilderness, and came to God's mountain, to Horeb. Yahweh's* angel appeared to him in a flame of fire out of the middle of a bush. He looked, and behold, the bush burned with fire, and the bush was not consumed. Moses said, "I will go now, and see this great sight, why the bush is not burned."

When Yahweh saw that he came over to see, God called to him out of the middle of the bush, and said, "Moses! Moses!"

He said, "Here I am."

He said, "Don't come close. Take off your sandals, for the place you are standing on is holy ground."

*Footnote ***Yahweh** is God's proper Name, sometimes rendered **LORD** (all caps) in other translations. WEB.*

Come into My presence and take off your old shoes for you too have come to a holy place of commissioning and setting forth. Your old shoes have served you well and brought you to this place; but you will need New Shoes of the Ruach HaKodesh that I'm offering you to fulfil the work that I have chosen for you. When you put them on you will hear My voice directing you more clearly than before. *Isaiah 30:21 Your ears will hear a word behind you, "This is the way, walk in it," whenever you turn to the right or to the left. AMP.*

Moses New Shoes directed him back to where he had come from; completely in the opposite direction he had been going most of his life. Jonah's New Shoes were on the beach when he was vomited up by the whale. Finally after running away from My commission he put on his New Shoes and set out for Nineveh.

Jonah 2:10 Then Yahweh spoke to the fish, and it vomited out Jonah on the dry land. WEB.

Jonah 3:1-5 Yahweh's word came to Jonah the second time, saying, "Arise, go to Nineveh, that great city, and preach to it the message that I give you."

So Jonah arose, and went to Nineveh, according to Yahweh's word. Now Nineveh was an exceedingly great city, three days' journey across. Jonah began to enter into the city a day's journey, and he cried out, and said, "In forty days, Nineveh will be overthrown!"

The people of Nineveh believed God; and they proclaimed a fast and put on sackcloth, from their greatest even to their least. WEB.

Many like yourself have absolutely no idea where I am directing you; but you are all prepared to put on your New Shoes willing to be led wherever I direct you; trusting Me with your future; having the full uncompromising assurance in your heart that wherever I send you it leads to Home. You know the destination; but you sense there is still a lot more adventures to be had in Me on the journey Home. I don't have a waiting room for you and others just to see out your time on earth!! I have adventures and fulfilment

7

and richness and spiritual wealth to release to you. Stop focusing on the negatives and what you lack. Look to Me and the wonderful provisions laid up for you and your loved ones until I bring you all safely Home to be with Me to be together for always.

The days are dark, but My bright eternal light is shining to direct your paths in these days of darkness and bring you all safely Home. It's time to put on your New Shoes.

CHAPTER 3
YAHWEH LOVES YOU

December 28th 2014; 6th Tevet 5775.

Yeshua Speaks: Yahweh Loves You with an everlasting love. His ways are past finding out and the manifestation of His great love for you is often misunderstood; for often a greater expression of love can only be released through what seems to you to be suffering or lack. The loving unseen hand of Abba often must direct you in unsavoury paths because of your hard heartedness or strong selfish motivations. As a wise loving Elohim He is not going to give you all the things that your heart desires; He knows full well you will soon become spoilt; enamoured with 'things' and your heart will turn from seeking to be with Him and spending time in His presence.

Your times of greatest needs are the times when He has turned your rebellious heart back to seeking the giver of all truly good gifts; your heavenly Abba. He is looking for the grateful heart that acknowledges that all things that happen to you and your families; both good and bad by your standards; are but the unseen loving hand at work guiding you into a covenant love relationship with the author of pure love and goodness.

Just as you discipline your own children; denying them certain foods, toys and 'things' that will harm their good nature so does your heavenly Abba dote on you; not allowing certain relationships with evil people to develop; not allowing you to pursue time-wasting activities that although may seem good on the surface; will not develop in you the godly character that He is nurturing.

Life's disappointments should lead you into a greater trust in Him who truly loves you; if you begin to open the eyes of your understanding you will see His loving hand has gently guided you into His perfect will; or to put it another way His very best for you; not only for the here and now; but for your future and the situations you will face in this lifetime. He wants you to have trust and faith in His abilities, His provision, His enabling, His great love for you; accepting that His is the greater wisdom at work in your life; leading and guiding you day by day into a loving covenant relationship.

Obey His mitzvot because this is the foundation of His love covenant. They are not rules to be obeyed in your own strength; they are guidelines that are to train and instruct you how to live a prosperous fulfilling life. A moments reflection will remind you that you cannot obey His commandments in your own strength because you have and always will fail; because it is only by His empowering and the actions of Ruach HaKodesh that you can begin to be pleasing to Him.

He is not an Elohim who is afar off. As you come to believe in and trust Him more and more; be willing to be led by His Ruach HaKodesh by sensitising yourself to His presence and His guidance; you will begin to experience

Yahweh's great love at a whole new level. Stop striving to please Him by doing things for Him; begin to allow Him to fill you with His good gifts; His nature, His patience, His compassion for others, His desire to allow His Ruach HaKodesh to guide you; particularly in your thought life and charitable unseen acts of kindness towards others.

Guard your heart against bitterness of the past; forgive and begin to thank your Abba in Heaven that through your wounds and suffering He brought and guided you back to sit at His feet sometimes broken and weeping; to ensure that His love could be released into your spirit to a far greater depth than you ever thought possible.

Deep wounds require deep healing and even Ruach HaKodesh surgery. Often it is those that wear the most scars that end up the most beautiful. A reflection of Abba's true love nature; accepting that it was He and He alone that rescued them from eternal death and separation from the author of creation, life and love; the true eternal covenant of love outlined in His holy Tanakh and B'rit Hadashah.

Insights: We are His adopted children and are entitled to all the covenant blessings reserved for His covenant children. We have entered into His love covenant by believing that He is who He says He is and does what He says He will do; incorporating the past, the present and the future. Even if we do not understand what He is doing in our lives we must come to have an absolute trust and faith in Him who knows the beginning and the end of all things.

We can be confident in His great love for us that did not hold back from laying all our sins and iniquities on His own precious Son; throwing them into the depths of the sea so that we could enjoy the benefits of His Kingdom; from here and all the way to infinity and beyond, never-ending, always new, always fresh. His is a Kingdom whose magnificence is beyond words and beyond the scope of our wildest imagination to comprehend. His great love and goodness is reserved for all who will by simple trust and faith enter into a trusting relationship with Him. Micah 7:19 *He will again have compassion on us. He will tread our iniquities under foot. You will cast all their sins into the depths of the sea. WEB.*

You ask; "How can I do this?" "Where do I start?" Just begin day by day to stop striving to work things out. Begin to trust Him in the little decisions; allowing the outcomes to be in the hands of His greater wisdom and power. Read and study the Tanakh for it is after all the record of the lives of ordinary people who stuffed up quite badly. Having destroyed their own lives, their careers, their kingships, their assignments, it was only Yahweh that brought them back on track guiding them with His loving hand.

They were all real people trying to do and become something in their own strength. Through their failures Yahweh demonstrated His power to rescue, to restore, to rehabilitate and honoured them and their stories for all time in the Holy Scriptures so that we could learn from their mistakes; begin to see plainly that the only answer to having a full and meaningful life is to find the one who is in control; not only of our lives, but all of mankind. In control of the earth, the heavens, the universe and all events past, present and future. He is the only one who can heal our hurts and wounds.

He is the only one that can cause us to be joyful and enjoy life in the midst of sorrows and sadness. It is He who can put a spring in our step and encourage us to sing songs to Him, even when we are chained up in prison. *Acts 16:22-25 The multitude rose up together against them and the magistrates tore their clothes from them, then commanded them to be beaten with rods. When they had laid many stripes on them, they threw them into prison, charging the jailer to keep them safely. Having received such a command, he threw them into the inner prison and secured their feet in the stocks.*

But about midnight Paul and Silas were praying and singing hymns to God, and the prisoners were listening to them. WEB.

It is He who can cause us to have His heart; forgiving people who are trying to harm us crying out to Him "Abba forgive them, for they know not what they are doing." *Acts 7:59-60 They stoned Stephen as he called out, saying, "Lord Jesus, receive my Spirit!" He kneeled down, and cried with a loud voice, "Lord, don 't hold this sin against them!" When he had said this, he fell asleep. WEB.*

With His help and the help of Ruach HaKodesh; we can and must move from being a victim of life; to begin one day at a time to learn how to walk victoriously through life's trials; acknowledging that they are not the real issue of life or a measure of success or failure; but simply the loving hand of Abba leading us into a deeper relationship with Him that very few find in this lifetime.

The Choice: Developing trust in Him is not easy, but it begins with a choice that says "no matter what happens, I will leave the outcome in Yahweh's hands. I will try not to get angry or disappointed with others' words and actions directed at me; I will, with His help, begin to forgive people for their actions and words that are hurtful or spiteful. I am on a journey to discover His great love for me and I recognise that it is often on the other side of suffering that I will enter into a deeper trust in Him; to appreciate His great and comprehensive love for me." Psalm 90:2 *Before the mountains were born, before you had formed the earth and the world, from eternity past to eternity future you are God. CJB.*

If Yeshua was perfected by His suffering and not spared

from persecution, hatred and a horrible death; we should be mindful that the journey that leads us closer to the very heart of a great loving Elohim could be a bumpy ride; often uncomfortable and unfair by our standards.

But His is the greater wisdom and His is the greater love that sees the end from the beginning; He always was and always will be watching lovingly over us, guiding us, correcting our ways; if necessary disciplining us knowing how we will turn out the moment before we step over into His eternal forever future.

Conclusion: Yahweh is shaping. Yahweh is refining. Yahweh is at work in your life. Stop blaming Him and appreciate and understand that He is drawing you to Himself in all that has happened in your life.

Look to His Word. Look to His Son. Look to His Ruach HaKodesh. Look for Him in all of life, each and every day!

Yahweh Loves You!

CHAPTER 4

CAVEAT

June 29th 2014; 1St Tamuz 5774.

Definition: to qualify a particular statement with a proviso. Definition of proviso: a condition, stipulation, provision, clause, rider, qualification, restriction, reservation, limitation or strings attached to an agreement or statement.

Yahweh Speaks: My word and My words to My children are without caveats. There is no hidden double meaning or added conditions or let-out or let-off clauses. My words are pure, undefiled, straightforward and plain. I say what I mean and I mean what I say. My words are forever words, settled in Heaven forever. *Psalm 119:89 Yahweh, your word is settled in heaven forever. WEB.*

From the time they are spoken they are surrounded with the power and glory to bring them to fulfilment and to maintain them forever. I speak things into existence. I created the world, the universe and mankind simply by speaking them into existence.

My creative energy surrounds My words and goes to bring it to completion; complying with My intuitive imagination. As I think and imagine and speak; so it is and so it will be. There is no limitation or hindrance to the fulfilling of My spoken word. That is who I Am, that is My power and My ability. My words are unalterable; they will achieve the purpose for which I sent them. They will be fulfilled and become fact and reality in your world; they are fact and reality the moment that I speak them here in My Kingdom. They are unstoppable; the glory and power released along with them will always bring them to fulfilment and completion.

Time is not a problem for Me as it is for you. Instantly for Me can be hundreds or thousands of years for you. The timing of the fulfilment is in My hands; My planning to bring all things together perfectly at the perfect time to satisfy Me and My plans for the establishment of the New Heavens and the New Earth. When My Son Yeshua came to your earth to rescue you from the adversary and provide a way of reconciliation with Myself it was the fulfilment of My word already declared in the heavens; it was accompanied by great power and glory needed for their fulfilment.

It is not over; the greater part of My salvation extends from the time I spoke My words covering hundreds and even thousands of years both sides of the short time My Son appeared on the earth. My words were not completed in the short 31 years He was on earth; they are being fulfilled every jot and tittle to their culmination and completion. All the redeemed will spend eternity here with Me, My beloved Son, My Ruach HaKodesh and a host of attending angels in a brand-new heaven and earth being formed even now to be ready right on time in the fulfilment of My perfect plans.

The disciples heard My words revealed and released to them by My Son and lived in a wonderful expectation that all that He spoke and revealed would surely come to pass. So real was this to them that they expected it to happen tomorrow in their time. They had My word and by experience they never doubted that I was able to do exactly as I said I would do. Their eyes were opened to the reality of the divine power and glory that accompany all of My words in the Tanakh and the Torah.

They looked with joyful expectation to the fulfilment of all and every word; they knew without the reserve of human reasoning that I could and would perform My words powerfully, wonderfully and supernaturally right in their midst. There was no doubting anymore; they had come through their time of unbelief and doubt after My Son was crucified. In their darkest hours I confirmed My word to them in the irrefutable miracle of life from death. The risen Messiah gave them the foundation and a rock-solid faith in every word My Son had spoken to them; the assurance and testimony in undeniable physical evidence that I am true to My word. They died not seeing the fulfilment in their world of all that I had spoken to them; but they died believing without a shadow of doubt that I am faithful, obedient and powerful to perform My words.

Through your difficult times you too will see My hand of deliverance, mercy and grace. You too like the early disciples; will no longer put faith in circumstances or anything in your physical world that contradicts My word. You will come to that inner assurance that even if you don't have any sign or wonder or miracle to affirm My words to you; you will remain rock solid in your dependence and absolute faith that I am true to My word; what I have spoken will come to pass in My perfect time and the time that is best for you and your circumstances. It is on its way. I have spoken it and it will not tarry. Believe it as fact. Count on it. Rejoice in the sure knowledge that I have spoken it and it will surely be.

As long as there is a heaven and an earth so shall My word prosper and blossom right on time and right in season. "Put Me in remembrance of My word" or more exactly, remind yourself of what I have spoken to you in My word; I have not forgotten. *Isaiah 43:26 Put me in remembrance. Let us plead together. Declare your case, that you may be justified. WEB.* This scripture is for your benefit. I will deliver everything I have spoken to you and all of My children; but you must allow Me the freedom and liberty to fulfil My promises My way; not limit Me to performing miracles, healings and miraculous provision in the narrow context of human reasoning. I have spoken and so it will be.

As simple and as powerful as this process is; you do not receive because you put limitations or caveats on My words. Because you do not receive an instant healing or find gold or jewels under your bed the morning after you prayed for financial blessings or for that matter your prayers seemed to go unanswered; you quickly put caveats on My word.

The main caveat that will hinder or stop My word being fulfilled in your life is the caveat of unbelief. You don't really believe that I can or will perform My word in your life. You may start out in powerful prayers even quoting My word; however because it is not answered quickly enough for you or circumstances tell you it was not answered you stop believing. You have put a caveat on My word!

The best response to your unbelief is to recognise unbelief for what it is. Confess it as sin and pray a simple honest prayer from your heart; "I do believe - deliver me from my unbelief." I can't deliver if you won't receive. Many parcels come back to Heaven marked *return to sender recipient will not take delivery.* Like Peter standing outside the house of praying believers after I had miraculously released him from prison; the answer to their prayers was standing at the door and they momentarily refused to accept and receive the answer to their prayers even though it was quite literally knocking on the door. *Acts 12:13-16 He knocked at the outside door, and a servant named Rhoda came to answer. She recognized Kefa's voice and was so happy that she ran back in without opening the door, and announced that Kefa was standing outside. "You're out of your mind!" they said to her. But she insisted it was true.*

So they said, "It is his angel." Meanwhile, Kefa kept knocking; and when they opened the door and saw him, they were amazed. CJB.

The Pharisees and the Torah experts and religious leaders rejected the answer to generations of prayer; unable to believe that the answer to their prayers was standing right in front of them; performing miracles, confirming and fulfilling My Word in the flesh. They rejected their Messiah because He wasn't what they expected. They discouraged the whole population from putting their trust in Yeshua; denying the validity of miracles performed before their very eyes; stirring up the crowds to support their unbelief. They crucified My answer to their prayers and sent Him back to Heaven refusing to take delivery of My Salvation.

The father who brought his son to be delivered stopped listening to the religious leaders and cried out "Lord I do believe you can set my son free; help me overcome my unbelief." *Mark 9:23-24 Jesus said to him, "If you can believe, all things are possible to him who believes." Immediately the father of the child cried out with tears, "I believe. Help my unbelief!" WEB.* His honest prayer was answered and his son was set free from the tormenting spirit.

Well did My Son identify the problem when He spoke to the religious leaders and the whole Jewish population of the day "People without any trust!" He responded. "How long will I be with you?" "How long must I put up with you?" I had spoken to that generation through My Son assuring them with signs and wonders that My authority over the powers of darkness was His and theirs too; if only they would believe and have faith in My Son; receive Him as their Messiah and grasp and own the fullness of My words spoken and revealed through Him. *Mark 9:19 "People without any trust!" he responded. "How long will I be with you? How long must I put up with you? Bring him to me!" CJB.*

Beware of the leaven of the Pharisees of your day that you, like them, will simply not believe and act on My promises; believing them as fact and reality. The power and authority that accomplish them is so because I have spoken it! Your caveat of unbelief does not lessen the power or authority of My promises and prophecies over your life; it simply prevents you from receiving them.

Yes it does disappoint and even exasperate Me, My Son and Ruach HaKodesh that you do without blessings and answers to your prayers because it wasn't fulfilled your way, in your timeframe or some other human fleshly reason.

I have spoken. I will deliver in My way, in My time, which by the way is the perfect timing for you also. Acknowledge and believe with a new assurance that I am for you, willing and able to perform My word in your life.

Remove the caveat of unbelief that is hindering My words blossoming in your life.

CHAPTER 5
THE GREATEST GIFT

John **3:16** *"For God so [greatly] loved and dearly prized the world, that He [even] gave His [One and] only begotten Son, so that whoever believes and trusts in Him [as Savior] shall not perish, but have eternal life. AMP.*

Yahweh Speaks: My Son Yeshua is My greatest gift to mankind. He is the way, the truth and the life that has been revealed to provide a doorway or an entrance into the Kingdom of Heaven. There is no other name given under heaven and there is no other way other than by knowing Him that will release the benefits of heaven to you. His name literally means Yahweh's salvation and it is through His obedient life that salvation has been, is being and will be released to all who will simply believe, accept and receive.

A gift cannot be earned. A priceless gift whose value is past finding out, that releases My very nature into your everyday situations to make you prosperous, wealthy and wise. A priceless jewel, a priceless wine; that will enable all who embrace it to experience a foretaste of heaven itself; the fullness of which will continue to be manifested in your life as you explore this most wonderful privilege. Blessings untold will unfold. Heaven's resources will be released as you treasure and develop the relationship with My Son that began as a free gift from My heart. *Isaiah 55:1 "All you who are thirsty, come to the water! You without money, come, buy, and eat! Yes, come! Buy wine and milk without money — it's free! CJB.*

Explore this gift and use it to open heavenly doors and walk by faith into the very chambers of Heaven itself. Experience first-hand the power and authority that is yours by the exercising of simple faith and belief in My great love for you and My willingness to share My glorious nature with you. Embrace the gift of My Son. Let it become a living breathing daily encounter that becomes more real than life itself. More real than things that you can touch and feel. Surer than the world's greatest treasures. Each day embrace My Son and I too will begin to embrace you as I embrace Him. My Ruach HaKodesh will gently guide you and assist you to understand how to best appropriate the gift of My Son.

Don't neglect My gift regarding it as some kind of insurance policy to gain entrance to My Heaven, but rather embrace it as the key that will open the very doorways of Heaven itself releasing all that I am to you here and now in your everyday life. I am alive, active and alert in your life on your behalf even when you are asleep. Believe this, receive and enjoy the benefits the gift of My Son have, are and will bestow on you every day you spend on earth and throughout eternity. Ever increasing, ever abundant, ever overflowing beyond your wildest imagination.

There is no limit to what My great gift to you will enable you to do for My glory; for your own enrichment; as you come to know My Son and Myself; as you explore all that He is and all that I AM. Bring the relationship with My Son that you have and that you are daily developing into My presence as led by My Spirit and see what I will do in your life as you handle, taste, embrace, explore, enjoy, treasure and daily fall deeper in love with My Son Yeshua – ***The Greatest Gift***

Romans 5:6-11 For while we were still helpless, at the right time, the Messiah died on behalf of ungodly people.

Now it is a rare event when someone gives up his life even for the sake of somebody righteous, although possibly for a truly good person one might have the courage to die.

But God demonstrates his own love for us in that the Messiah died on our behalf while we were still sinners.

Therefore, since we have now come to be considered righteous by means of his bloody sacrificial death, how much more will we be delivered through him from the anger of God's judgment!

For if we were reconciled with God through his Son's death when we were enemies, how much more will we be delivered by his life, now that we are reconciled!

And not only will we be delivered in the future, but we are boasting about God right now, because he has acted through our Lord Yeshua the Messiah, through whom we have already received that reconciliation. CJB.

CHAPTER 6
CALAMITY

January 12th 2015; 21st Tevet 5775.

Definition: an event causing great and often sudden damage or distress; a disaster.

Yahweh Speaks: There is a season of Calamity that is soon to come upon the world. It will come without warning at its appointed time which is known beforehand only by Me. The prophets of old have warned you of these days; it is in My plans to wind up the affairs of wicked men; to expose the powers of darkness that have remained hidden throughout the ages.

Many cataclysmic events will begin to explode all around the world with such intensity and destructive force that unless I shorten these days of calamity the whole earth would be destroyed.

Daniel 9:7-14 "To you, Adonai, belongs righteousness; but to us today belongs shame — to us, the men of Y'hudah, the inhabitants of Yerushalayim and all Isra'el, including those nearby and those far away, throughout all the countries where you have driven them; because they broke faith with you.

Yes, Adonai, shame falls on us, our kings, our leaders and our ancestors; because we sinned against you. It is for Adonai our God to show compassion and forgiveness, because we rebelled against him. We didn't listen to the voice of Adonai our God, so that we could live by his laws, which he presented to us through his servants the prophets.

Yes, all Isra'el flouted your Torah and turned away, unwilling to listen to your voice. Therefore the curse and oath written in the Torah of Moshe the servant of God was poured out on us, because we sinned against him.

He carried out the threats he spoke against us and against our judges who judged us, by bringing upon us disaster so great that under all of heaven, nothing has been done like what has been done to Yerushalayim.

As written in the Torah of Moshe, this whole disaster came upon us. Yet we did not appease Adonai our God by renouncing our wrongdoing and discerning your truth.

So Adonai watched for the right moment to bring this disaster upon us, for Adonai our God was just in everything he did, yet we didn't listen when he spoke. CJB.

You will have stripped away all that you have put your faith and confidence in; money, wealth, possessions, houses, earthly governments, armies and weapons. Nothing will protect you from what is about to befall the earth. There is no person or government that you can turn to, to save you in these desperate days and you must trust Me as never before. I will sustain you; I will provide for you, I will protect you through these dark and desperate times.

Many will lose their loved ones; their livelihood and their loss will be unbearable for them. They will turn in anger towards Me and begin to vent their fury at all who survive and seem to suffer little or no loss. They will call Me a cruel and sadistic uncaring God because they have never taken any time in their lives to get to know Me or even to

25

seek to know Me. In these days some so-called Christians will also turn their backs on Me; do not be surprised when members of the Christian family rail against you right along with the rest of the world.

I am the God of truth, justice and righteousness. My judgments on the earth will be exacerbated by the evil men who have manipulated the weather, created sophisticated weapons of mass destruction, mined the surfaces of the earth, exploded atomic devices deep within the crust of the earth; all for their desire to gain control over the earth's population and destructively plunder the earths riches; storing them all up for themselves and the elite few. There are angels in the abyss who were bound and sent there for future judgment who practiced the same evils. Did you think that I would indefinitely stay My hand when the blood of generations of innocents slain by evil men and evil powers of darkness driving them is crying out to Me to the very throne room of Heaven for justice?

My scriptures tell of the day when the cup of My wrath will be filled to overflowing and My final judgments will be poured out upon the earth. My judgments and the war to end all wars are measured and limited; so that even in My judgments of the earth and all of mankind there always remains the opportunity for My mercy and grace to be extended to all who will reach out to Me in the coming dark and desperate hours. Right to the very end My hand is extended to all who will turn from the power of the adversary and cry out to Me to save them not only from the calamity of these days but from eternal death and damnation.

Matthew 24:3-14 When he was sitting on the Mount of Olives, the talmidim came to him privately. "Tell us," they said, "when will these things happen? And what will be the sign that you are coming, and that the 'olam hazeh is ending?"

Yeshua replied: "Watch out! Don't let anyone fool you! For many will come in my name, saying, 'I am the Messiah!' and they will lead many astray. You will hear the noise of wars nearby and the news of wars far off; see to it that you don't become frightened. Such things must happen, but the end is yet to come. For peoples will fight each other, nations will fight each other, and there will be famines and earthquakes in various parts of the world; all this is but the beginning of the 'birth-pains.'

At that time you will be arrested and handed over to be punished and put to death, and all peoples will hate you because of me. At that time many will be trapped into betraying and hating each other, many false prophets will appear and fool many people; and many people's love will grow cold because of increased distance from Torah. But whoever holds out till the end will be delivered.

And this Good News about the Kingdom will be announced throughout the whole world as a witness to all the Goyim. It is then that the end will come. CJB.

Some of you will not survive these days and you need to get your hearts and minds ready to be swept into My presence. Those who do survive I will protect and provide for and hide in secret places. I will endue you with power to survive so that you can be witnesses and a testimony to those whose hearts are still open to receive Me. Many will want to kill you as they did the apostles of old; but I will enable, protect and empower you to fulfil My plans and purposes in your life to survive this season.

Revelation 6:9-11 When he opened the fifth seal, I saw underneath the altar the souls of those who had been killed for the Word of God, and for the testimony of the Lamb which they had.

They cried with a loud voice, saying, "How long, Master, the holy and true, until you judge and avenge our blood on those who dwell on the earth?"

A long white robe was given to each of them. They were told that they should rest yet for a while, until their fellow servants and their brothers, who would also be killed even as they were, should complete their course. WEB.

Like a raging bushfire some will be spared loss and some will lose all; you will have no control over these events. Be warned that these days are coming soon and prepare your hearts to be led by Ruach HaKodesh. Re-evaluate your lives while there is still time and draw close to Me as never before.

Yeshua Speaks: I am the Good Shepherd of the flock of Abba and I will protect you as you look in sheep like faith to Me as your redeemer, saviour, provider, guide, protector and enabler.

Come into the fold of Abba's love and He will lead and guide you as He always has through this coming calamity.

Psalm 91 He who dwells in the secret place of the Most High will rest in the shadow of the Almighty.

I will say of Yahweh, "He is my refuge and my fortress; my God, in whom I trust."

For he will deliver you from the snare of the fowler, and from the deadly pestilence.

He will cover you with his feathers. Under his wings you will take refuge. His faithfulness is your shield and rampart.

You shall not be afraid of the terror by night, nor of the arrow that flies by day; nor of the pestilence that walks in darkness, nor of the destruction that wastes at noonday.

A thousand may fall at your side, and ten thousand at your right hand; but it will not come near you.

You will only look with your eyes, and see the recompense of the wicked.

Because you have made Yahweh your refuge, and the Most High your dwelling place, no evil shall happen to you, neither shall any plague come near your dwelling.

For he will put his angels in charge of you, to guard you in all your ways.

They will bear you up in their hands, so that you won't dash your foot against a stone.

You will tread on the lion and cobra. You will trample the young lion and the serpent underfoot.

"Because he has set his love on me, therefore I will deliver him. I will set him on high, because he has known my name.

He will call on me, and I will answer him. I will be with him in trouble. I will deliver him, and honor him.

I will satisfy him with long life, and show him my salvation."
WEB.

CHAPTER 7

BLESSING SANDWICHES

A Modern-Day Parable!

February 8th 2015; 19th Sh'vat 5775. There was a little girl in the school playground who shared her sandwiches and treats with everybody. She was a very happy little girl who loved to share with others. Her father was a sandwich maker in the local shop and he too was very generous toward his customers. He was very proud of his daughter because she had inherited his generous spirit.

One day there came some bullies into the playground who were jealous of all the sandwiches and treats the little girl always had; they came over to her and took all her sandwiches and treats and made fun of her and embarrassed her in front of all the other children. They gave her back one sandwich and one small chocolate bar and said "That's all you'll need, we will keep the rest safely under lock and key so that no one will steal them from you." They laughed mockingly and walked away, hurling abuse and threatened her to stop giving away any more sandwiches and treats or they would be back.

The little girl was in tears and when she told her father

he comforted her and said; "I have plenty more sandwiches and you will never want and you will always have more than enough to give away and share with others." The little girl went back to the school playground; at first she was terrified; the threatening words of the bullies were still ringing in her ears. As time went by she overcame her fears and she developed many friends who loved her for who she was and not just for the sandwiches she gave them. They got to know her father as well; he treated them generously as if they were his own children and would often give them special treats on their way home from school. The playground was a happy joyful place for all who came there.

Then one day the bullies came back and surrounded the little girl. "Oh you have come to give back the sandwiches you took" she said. "I'm glad you came as there are now many more children in the playground who need feeding." The bullies said "Come to give them back? You must be joking, we've eaten all those and we need more. Give us all your sandwiches and treats right now!" They proceeded to push and jostle her, and took not only her sandwiches but also all the sandwiches and treats she had given to the other children. "You can't take those!" the little girl protested; "My daddy made them especially for me to give away!" "What are you going to do about it you little pipsqueak?" said the bullies. She stood her ground and all the children in the playground stood up one by one and began to stand behind her until the whole playground was standing and they advanced towards the bullies.

The bullies backed away but continued to threaten and yell; "this is your last warning, stop sharing these sandwiches and giving them away. They are ours. You have no right to them, and what are you going to do about it anyway, you and your loser friends?"

There was silence for a moment and then laughter erupted across the playground. The bullies were perplexed but made threatening gesticulations and turned to go away with the stolen sandwiches; but unbeknown to them and blocking their way was the little girl's father and his helpers standing with their arms folded right behind them!

"Going somewhere?" the father asked. The bullies were caught red handed still holding the sandwiches and treats in their hands they stood frozen in their tracks. The father blocked their path and looking them straight in the eye he said "You wicked children; all you had to do was ask me and I would have given you all the sandwiches you needed. But since you have chosen to steal what rightfully belongs to others things will not go well with you from this very day. The sandwiches that I make for my daughter are for giving away and sharing. They are called Blessing Sandwiches; they bless those that give them away and they bless those that receive them with thankful hearts. Since you have stolen them to keep for yourselves, they will go rotten in your mouths because my Blessings Sandwiches are made for sharing and blessing others in need. Now be on your way; take the sandwiches you have stolen and never let me catch you in this playground ever again! The sandwiches that I had planned to give to you will be given to others."

"Listen up all you good and faithful children gathered in this playground; I have fresh sandwiches and treats for you all and I am inviting you to have afternoon tea with me and my daughter in my shop after school."

The playground erupted in shouts of joy and squeals of delight as the bullies slunk away with their ill-gotten spoils.

CHAPTER 8

RIGHTEOUSNESS

F ebruary 2nd 2015; 13th Sh'vat 5775. What does it mean to be righteous and to have righteousness? Is it our own righteousness that makes us more acceptable to Yahweh? Well scripture plainly tells us that this is not so; clearly stating that no one is righteous. *Ecclesiastes 7:20 Surely there is not a righteous man on earth who does good and doesn't sin. WEB.*

How then can we be righteous or in right standing with Yahweh? Is it a path or journey that we follow; obeying religious rules so that someday, somehow, we might arrive at a righteous state that is acceptable to Almighty God? The Bible illustrates clearly that despite man's best efforts to approach the author and source of righteousness; we will always fall short.

In the Tanakh the sin sacrifices covered man's shortcomings; they covered their unrighteousness by annually appointing innocent animals to pay the penalty for their sins and atone for their unrighteousness. The annual sacrifices that cost the lives of innocent animals clearly spoke of a severe shortcoming or gap between our ancestors' righteousness and the Righteousness of Yahweh.

The sacrifices were a foreshadowing of the perfect sacrifice of God's own Son Yeshua; whose sinless blood covered our sins and allowed us to be clothed in Yahweh's Righteousness for the first time in history. The Righteousness of Messiah, or more exactly the righteous nature of Yahweh present in His Son Yeshua; allowed Yahweh to look upon us as being righteous in His sight; because the cloak of Righteousness that belongs to Yeshua makes us acceptable and able to fellowship and have an ongoing relationship with Yeshua, Yahweh and the indwelling Ruach HaKodesh.

By faith in Yeshua; simply believing that Yahweh came in the flesh; His own Son taking on and being in human form; we can enter into His Righteousness. It always has been an entering into His Righteousness; accessed by believing and trusting in His Son Yeshua; that we experience this wonderful righteousness.

Its source is Heaven itself and it is Abba's heart to make us acceptable in His eyes so that He can fellowship and communicate with us all the wonderful things that He wants to share with us.

Romans 3:20-26 For in his sight no one alive will be considered righteous on the ground of legalistic observance of Torah commands, because what Torah really does is show people how sinful they are.

But now, quite apart from Torah, God's way of making people righteous in his sight has been made clear — although the Torah and the Prophets give their witness to it as well — and it is a righteousness that comes from God, through the faithfulness of Yeshua the Messiah, to all who continue trusting. For it makes no difference whether one is a Jew or a Gentile, since all have sinned and come short of earning God's praise.

By God's grace, without earning it, all are granted the status of being considered righteous before him, through the act redeeming us from our enslavement to sin that was accomplished by the Messiah Yeshua.

God put Yeshua forward as the kapparah for sin through his faithfulness in respect to his bloody sacrificial death. This vindicated God's righteousness; because, in his forbearance, he had passed over [with neither punishment nor remission] the sins people had committed in the past;

and it vindicates his righteousness in the present age by showing that he is righteous himself and is also the one who makes people righteous on the ground of Yeshua's faithfulness. CJB.

Heaven is full of resources, abilities, protection and provision for all who have the righteous nature of Abba surrounding them. Righteousness is not a feeling and it is not about us feeling righteous; it is a foundational principle of the Kingdom. Kingdom dwellers are covered with a cloak of righteousness - a protective covering; as the scripture says "Put on righteousness for a breastplate." His Righteousness so that when the evil day comes we will clearly have faith in Him and not our religious selves. Many have accomplished and achieved great things for the Kingdom; these achievements are because of Yahweh's Righteousness that is at work in the earth. *Ephesians 6:14 Therefore, stand! Have the belt of truth buckled around your waist, put on righteousness for a breastplate. CJB.*

Never get puffed up with works - even works for Him and the Kingdom; foolish pride in our spirituality and achievements will lead us into the error of thinking that it was somehow because of our righteousness that Yahweh gave us a special dispensation. No and doubly no!

Many servants of God became deceived and puffed up

because God was using them so mightily; they fell from grace some quite spectacularly. When we are in touch with Him through His Ruach HaKodesh; His Righteousness permeates our very being.

It is time to humbly recognise that He has been gracious to us and allowed His righteous favour to be extended to us for the achieving of His purposes; not ours. We are not owed His Righteousness and it is not some kind of badge of honour for services rendered. It is at His volition and He can pour out or measure His holy Righteousness as it suits Him and never us. Be attentive and wise to His dealings with you on this matter. It is not about feelings, but rather that inner assurance that He is in control and can at any time increase or decrease the operation of His Righteousness in our lives. Walk humbly in the shadow of the Almighty; humble yourself often in His presence; thanking Him for all His goodness and good pleasure released to you and your loved ones.

Yahweh is no man's debtor and the good gifts He bestows on us are a reflection of His Righteousness; which was and is only made available to us by a simple trust and belief that He alone is the author and provider of access to His Righteousness; which is who He is and who His Son Yeshua is.

In closing always remember that His Righteousness cannot be earned or attained to by the observance of religious practices. It is a free gift from Abba's heart, so that we can fellowship and commune with Him in Heaven whilst still on earth. The full measure of His glory and Righteousness cannot be tolerated by our human bodies; it is only when we are translated or transformed into our new spiritual bodies that we can stand to be in the near presence of the righteous ones, Yahweh and Yeshua and the glory that surrounds them, permeating and radiating from their very beings. *Galatians 5:4-5 You who are trying to be declared righteous by God through legalism have severed yourselves from the Messiah! You have fallen away from God's grace! For it is by the power of the Spirit, who works in us because we trust and are faithful, that we confidently expect our hope of attaining righteousness to be fulfilled. CJB.*

So enjoy His Righteousness as it comes upon you and do all to remain humble and thankful; remembering that it is His Righteousness released in measure to you whom He loves and adores; so that as Yeshua prayed we may be one with Abba as He is one with Him; enjoying all the attributes of the family of believers that He intended for us to enjoy. Every perfect and good gift comes from Abba's heart. Receive by faith the gift of His Righteousness and explore it as Ruach HaKodesh leads you.

His Righteousness is for the savouring and experiencing and will draw you closer to Him. It is His nature and He created you in His image so that you can be complete in coming to know Him. *John 17:21 that they may all be one. Just as you, Father, are united with me and I with you, I pray that they may be united with us, so that the world may believe that you sent me. CJB.*

Righteousness is not a feeling; often you will enter into a righteous state unawares; it will only be in hindsight that you will recognise a season in your life where you felt He was especially close to you or you close to Him and His righteous nature had touched you. You don't have to seek it or endeavour to find it; His nature, His love, His holiness, His glory and His Righteousness will touch you here in this lifetime until we are all in His presence where He can finally reveal to us the fullness of who He is.

All the glorious, righteous, holy moments of His divine

presence that we experience in our lives are but a tiny fore-taste of what He has prepared and laid up for all who love Him with a pure undefiled heart. Keep your hearts pure; accepting the wonderful intimate times when we knew beyond a shadow of a doubt that He was touching us and reassuring us that we are His not only for now in this life-time; but for ever and ever.

We must become like Him if we are to know and experi-ence His full wonderful nature but that will not be here on earth; it is reserved for all those who remain faithful to the end.

There are tough times coming; but His Righteousness and His righteous favour will protect, guide and lead us until we go Home to be with Him forever. It is time to go explore, invite, savour and enjoy His Righteousness as it comes our way.

CHAPTER 9
FORTITUDE

March 7th 2015; 16th Adar 5775.

Definition: strength of mind that enables a person to encounter danger or bear pain or adversity with courage.

Ruach HaKodesh Speaks: There is a time for remaining silent and there is a time for taking a stand for righteousness. We are fast moving into a season of persecution and ribald unrighteousness being released at all levels. It is a time to stand firm in your beliefs and begin to lay in place your own stronghold of relationship with Me. It is I who will give you the fortitude to stand up and speak up for what is just and holy and righteous in these days of deteriorating values at all levels in your society.

I will teach you how to speak truth into the situations that are confronting by nature. Never has the society you live in needed more men and women of integrity to stand against the wicked deterioration of all the values that made your culture and way of life strong and stable, than it does now.

Your leaders are bending to the power being exerted on

them by minority groups; they so greatly fear being removed from office. They are being stripped of meaningful authority and are being moulded into society's whims and an insatiable appetite for control of the public purse.

Godless men and women are taking control of your society; dictating to all false values based solely on convenience and keeping them in power. Marriage and the value of life are two foundational issues that are being sacrificed on the political altar and should be a harbinger that your society is crumbling. Perversion, weakness of leadership, corruption on a grand scale and victimisation is all a part of the times that you live in.

As your leaders continue to turn their backs on biblical values and the God of the universe and His Righteousness, and righteous instructions; they will bring your nation down with them. Corruption does come from the top and you should be praying that those of your leaders who are righteous will exert their influence in their portfolios; that they will have the fortitude to do what is right by the people of the nation and not act in their own political self-interest. There are some in your government who are My sons and daughters; the overwhelming political pressure that is being placed on them by the elite few can sway them from their own belief system; for the good of their political party's survival.

Yahweh Speaks: You too as My sons and daughters will come under increased pressure to compromise your beliefs and maintain all that you have worked for. It is time to prepare for the days that are coming; begin to steel yourselves against the deteriorating values of the society you live in. Stand up for what is right, righteous, holy and noble and the values that come from the Kingdom of Heaven. You have lived in a time of peace and were able to live a quiet and comfortable life without your core values coming under attack; be warned that the world and your society is changing and great injustices will begin to fall on all who are called by My name.

There will be no escape for Jews and Christians and the values that you all hold so dear; the god of this world has begun his final challenge to My authority as he has always done. There is nowhere to hide anymore; you and your loved ones will soon find yourselves on the firing line and you may be targeted by the evil one through one of his many wicked schemes. As I said to Joshua; "Be strong, be bold don't be afraid or downhearted, because Yahweh your God is with you wherever you go." *Joshua 1:9 Haven't I ordered you, 'Be strong, be bold'? So don't be afraid or downhearted, because ADONAI your God is with you wherever you go. CJB.*

I will give you the fortitude you will need to live through the days that even now are coming upon you. The only thing that is certain about these times is that everything is uncertain. I am about to shake this world and everything that can be shaken will be shaken.

You are living in the last days and your hearts and lives will be tested. Your allegiance to Me and to others of the household of faith will be tested; but know that I am standing with you and yours. *Luke 21:25-28 "There will appear signs in the sun, moon and stars; and on earth, nations will be in anxiety and bewilderment at the sound and surge of the sea, as people faint with fear at the prospect of what is overtaking the world; for the powers in heaven will be shaken.*

And then they will see the Son of Man coming in a cloud with tremendous power and glory. When these things start to happen, stand up and hold your heads high; because you are about to be liberated!" CJB.

I will release courage, bravery, wisdom, provision and protection as I have often told you. Do not be afraid of their faces as they are only the devil's spokesmen; pawns in his hands desperately trying to preserve their way of life, their possessions, their power and will stop at nothing to retain and maintain their advantage. These are desperate times that you live in but they are exciting times too; you will be drawn closer to Me and the relationship that is born in times of tribulation and suffering is a bond that has a depth that cannot be expressed in words.

"Wide, wide as the ocean, high as the heaven above; Deep, deep as the deepest sea is my Saviour's love. I, though so unworthy, still am a child of His care; For His Word teaches me that His love reaches me everywhere." Charles A Miles 1914.

Romans 8:35-39 Who will separate us from the love of the Messiah? Trouble? Hardship? Persecution? Hunger? Poverty? Danger? War?

As the Tanakh puts it, "For your sake we are being put to death all day long, we are considered sheep to be slaughtered."

No, in all these things we are super conquerors, through the one who has loved us.

For I am convinced that neither death nor life, neither angels nor other heavenly rulers, neither what exists nor what is coming, neither powers above nor powers below, nor any other created thing will be able to separate us from the love of God which comes to us through the Messiah Yeshua, our Lord. CJB.

I never called you to do that which you were unable to do. I never send you into battles unless I have equipped you and you are ready. It is your testimony and the blood of the Lamb that overcomes the evil one. Remember all the good and wonderful things I have done for you in our walk together. Draw aside often with Me and spend time in the word and allow Ruach HaKodesh to strengthen and steel your spirit for these days.

It is a battle that has already been won so don't strive to be strong in yourself; your true strength comes from the relationship you have with Me. Strive to enter into the rest that a strong relationship with Me gives you. Be confident in the strength that I will give you and not your own. You are promoting My righteousness and My values, not your own; so relax the buck stops with Me.

Yeshua Speaks: It is Me, Yahweh, Ruach HaKodesh, the bible, the Jews, the land of Israel and all that I have done and spoken that the devil has the problem with. You can only honestly speak out, act out and live out the benefits that I have extended to you; simply because you believed My words, accepted Me as your Saviour, your Lord, your King, your adviser, your everything and have lived your life to please Me and honour Me.

Your life is your testimony; the words of your testimony only seal and confirm your belief in Me and My goodness, kindness, provision, mercy and grace extended to you here on this earth. *Revelation 12:11 "They defeated him because of the Lamb's blood and because of the message of their witness. Even when facing death they did not cling to life. CJB.*

The experiences you have had in this lifetime are but a foretaste of what is laid up for you and all who love Me; all who will be My faithful disciples and children till the end of your days on earth. Don't despair when the evil day comes for I am with you as I have spoken and promised so many times in My word. Evil will draw near and try to oppress you but as you stand and allow Me to guide you; the evil presence will not overwhelm you or destroy you.

You will need My Fortitude to resist the evil one in the evil days that lay ahead. Rest in Me; develop a relationship with Me. Eat My flesh, drink My blood for these are your supernatural provision to equip and sustain you. (Refer to Keep The Charge of the Lord - Season Seven; Above The Line Thinking.)

John 6:53-56 Then Yeshua said to them, "Yes, indeed! I tell you that unless you eat the flesh of the Son of Man and drink his blood, you do not have life in yourselves.

Whoever eats my flesh and drinks my blood has eternal life — that is, I will raise him up on the Last Day. For my flesh is true food, and my blood is true drink. Whoever eats my flesh and drinks my blood lives in me, and I live in him. CJB.

The earth is entering into the final judgment season and Satan is causing all of his evil cohorts to seduce mankind into joining his rebellion against Yahweh, His Ruach HaKodesh and Me His Son. It will be a brutal bloody time that will embrace the whole world. His true evil nature will be revealed in its fullness before the courts of Heaven; this great evil will be revealed for all to see why My eternal judgment and eternal torment in the Lake of Fire is a just and righteous judgment.

Fear not the days of evil for as terrible as they will be; they will be cut short by My hand. It is a time to stand up and be counted as being on My side; for justice, truth, righteousness and My coming Kingdom. *1 Chronicles 12:17-18 David went out to meet them, and answered them," If you have come peaceably to me to help Me, My heart will be united with you; but if you have come to betray me to my adversaries, since there is no wrong in my hands, may the God of our fathers see this and rebuke it."*

Then the Spirit came on Amasai, who was chief of the thirty, and he said, "We are yours, David, and on your side, you son of Jesse. Peace, peace be to you, and peace be to your helpers; for your God helps you." Then David received them, and made them captains of the band. WEB.

Who is on the Lords side? Frances R. Havergal 1877.

Who is on the Lord's side? Who will serve the King? Who will be His helpers, other lives to bring?

Who will leave the world's side? Who will face the foe? Who is on the Lord's side? Who for Him will go?

By Thy call of mercy, by Thy grace divine, We are on the Lord's side—Saviour, we are Thine!

Not for weight of glory, nor for crown and palm, Enter we the army, raise the warrior psalm;

But for love that claimeth lives for whom He died: He whom Jesus saveth marches on His side.

By Thy love constraining, by Thy grace divine, We are on the Lord's side—Saviour, we are Thine!

Jesus, Thou hast bought us, not with gold or gem, But with Thine own lifeblood, for Thy diadem;

With Thy blessing filling each who comes to Thee, Thou hast made us willing, Thou hast made us free.

By Thy grand redemption, by Thy grace divine, We are on the Lord's side—Savior, we are Thine!

Fierce may be the conflict, strong may be the foe, But the King's own army none can overthrow;

'Round His standard ranging, vict'ry is secure, For His truth unchanging makes the triumph sure.

Joyfully enlisting, by Thy grace divine, We are on the Lord's side—Savior, we are Thine!

Chosen to be soldiers, in an alien land, Chosen, called, and faithful, for our Captain's band;

In the service royal, let us not grow cold, Let us be right loyal, noble, true and bold.

Master, wilt Thou keep us, by Thy grace divine, Always on the Lord's side—Savior, always Thine!

None can wrest you from My strong hand that is upon you. Do not go to be a watchman on the wall and spend energy and time looking at what the enemy is doing. It is a wrong focus. Like Elisha the prophet lock yourself away with Me; look on My face and draw strength from My glorious presence; when it is time to confront the evil one you will find that just like Elisha, I went before him; defeated the enemy that was besieging them and simply gave him the words to declare to the king and the people who were terrified by the imminent threat of annihilation "By this time tomorrow the enemy will be defeated."

2 Kings 7:1-2 Then Elisha said, "Hear the word of the Lord. Thus says the Lord, 'Tomorrow about this time a measure of finely-milled flour will sell for a shekel, and two measures of barley for a shekel, at the gate of Samaria.'"

Then the royal officer on whose arm the king leaned answered the man of God and said, "If the Lord should make windows in heaven [for the rain], could this thing take place?" Elisha said, "Behold, you will see it with your own eyes, but [because you doubt] you will not eat of it." AMP.

Come now into My presence; let Me give you a measure of My Divine Fortitude.

CHAPTER 10

TRIBULATION

March 16th 2015; 25th Adar 5775.

Definition: an experience that tests one's endurance, patience or faith.

There are many trials and tribulations that we will face in our lifetime. They are all very personal and almost tailor-made to test us at the point of our greatest vulnerability. Tribulations are one of life's greatest equalisers. The wealthy, the strong, the brave, the weak, the timid, can all alike face what is for them a terrible tailor-made tribulation. Those that have always enjoyed wealth are greatly thrown off base in times of lack or periods of poverty. The strong physically are greatly challenged by the loss of their strength through sickness or injury. Popular people who suddenly are judged as being morally reprehensible particularly through the lies of jealous peers; find great difficulty coming to terms with the shame; either real or imagined that they are now enduring.

In times of tribulation all falsehoods are exposed; false values, false friends, false faith, false expectations, false beliefs, marriage and family breakdowns; because they all come under the scrutiny of life stripped bare of all pretence; exposed in a raw, cold, cruel and uncomfortable tumultuous emotional storm; which can leave us isolated for a season; shipwrecked, abandoned and stranded on a lonely deserted island. A timeless introspection of all that represents our life; our values and our beliefs threaten to be our undoing and torments us. Everything has gone pearshaped; death, sickness, tragedy, loss all implode on us threatening to destroy our life's values, our future, our loves; they all become mixed up in some crazy neverending nightmare. *"When will it end, this inner torment?"* *"What can I do?"* *"What decision do I need to make?"*

There is not a clear path forward now that all my dreams have been shattered. All that I have held dear and put my total faith and trust in has abandoned me in my greatest hour of need. All the things I used to do like quoting scripture, praying every morning, singing songs of praise and worship feel like lumps of lead pulling me down further into my personal hell of desperation and hopelessness. Voices cry out from my innermost being questioning everything that I have ever believed and put my trust in.

The inner thoughts rise up:

"Why was I ever born?"

"Who am I really?"

"Who is God?"

"Am I really born again?"

"Why can't I feel anything?"

"Why am I so numb?"

"Is everything that I've ever believed just been one big lie - a hoax by an unseen spiritual power?"

"Why do I find myself in this tribulation?"

"Was it something that I said or did wrong?"

"It's like a quagmire, the more I struggle and try to get free,

the deeper I sink into my unanswered dilemmas. Staring wide-eyed into the night, trying to calm my raging fears and inner torment."

"How did this happen?"

"I don't know when it started and I see no end in sight."

"There is no answer, no solution, and no salvation in sight, just an inner knowing that I must somehow continue on until my time of tribulation ends or is miraculously resolved."

"I need to overcome it or it will overcome me!"

Reality Check: Tribulation is very personal and it is like standing naked before the creator of the universe stripped of all of your life's supports. There is nowhere to hide and your secret thoughts scream out from your innermost being. You are often shocked by what you are thinking and planning to do; knowing that nothing is hidden anymore and the shocking realisation that you have harboured resentment against so many people and even God Himself.

The revelation is a brutal confrontation with the real you warts and all; all that has lived hidden deep within your soul. This is the end of the charade that you have been living. Reality is dawning that your motives have never been pure. The shadow lands you have lived in have just had the spotlight of Heaven directed onto them. No more pretence, no more lies, nowhere to hide; just you standing in the presence of Yahweh the Creator of the universe the creator of you; finally acknowledging your sinful state when exposed to His glorious presence and His pure righteous holiness. You can fight it; you can come up with a plan of action but ultimately you will be confronted with the stark reality; your sinful self standing in the presence of Pure Love.

So here you are alone and stripped bare of all pretence standing in the loving presence of Abba who is wanting to embrace you with His Great Love; to guide you not only through this time of tribulation; but for always.

The truth of relationship with a holy righteous, glorious all-powerful Spirit entity is dawning on your spirit. It is only as you allow Him to possess you body, mind and spirit that you can have the deep meaningful relationship you have always desired; but never known how to initiate or make a reality in your life. Your tribulation will lead you to accept and allow Him to infuse and permeate all of you; to allow Him the freedom to direct your every thought and action from here to eternity and beyond. You can of course draw back and refuse Him the free and open access that He desires and handle your time of tribulation in your own strength; He will never act against your free will. It is your choice.

Tribulation is your opportunity to lay down your life, your desires, your sense of justice, your unforgiveness, especially of yourself and will allow you to cross over a new threshold in your life; becoming and experiencing the truth of the scripture that says it is "No longer I that lives, but Messiah that now lives within me by His Ruach HaKodesh." *Galatians 2:20 When the Messiah was executed on the stake as a criminal, I was too; so that my proud ego no longer lives. But the Messiah lives in me, and the life I now live in my body I live by the same trusting faithfulness that the Son of God had, who loved me and gave himself up for me. CJB.*

It begins with your choice and choosing each day to reinforce that choice by forgiving all those that seek to harm you or gain an advantage over you. He will change you from the inside out until His Ruach HaKodesh resides within you; and you're able to say with genuineness of spirit, "Abba forgive them for they know not what they are doing" to all who have brought you into your time of tribulation. *Luke 23:34a Yeshua said, "Father, forgive them; they don't understand what they are doing."…. CJB.*

On the other side tribulation is a newfound love for Yeshua, Yahweh and Ruach HaKodesh. There will be a flowing together as you stand on the basis of the newfound relationship that was forged in hours of desperation, tears and agonising of spirit. Deep calls unto deep and tribulation will bring you face-to-face with Yahweh; who will strip you of the burial garments that Satan has dressed you in and clothe you in new bright and cheerful garments of praise and gratitude.

Take up the mantle offered to you and your heart will leap for joy whenever you sense He is near. No longer be fearful running away from Him but always to Him; depending on Him for every new breath of life.

The panacea for your sins, past, present and future is always found in Abba's presence and you need to have confidence in Yeshua, Yahweh's salvation; and be confident in your right to be one of His sons or daughters; knowing that all your shortcomings and failures are under the blood of the Lamb. He desires a relationship with you that will enrich, empower, encourage, excite and enthuse you each and every day. Every day is a new and exciting adventure in Him; you are to live in the wonderful expectation that He is looking for you each day.

Get into the habit of talking to Him. Devour His instructions to you contained in His word. Look for Him in all of life. Change your glasses; look through the glasses of Heaven and stop being intimidated by everyday events; especially when bad things seem to happen. Become aware that He is leading, guiding and protecting you and all your loved ones in these last days.

Yahweh Speaks: Look up and live! Stop looking around

and down because these events will cause you to have a wrong focus. Stop being so negative in your thinking and begin to look for My positives in all that happens to you and seek to accept and receive life as a blessing from My hand.

Tribulation will bring you back on track and as difficult as it is to bear: your season of tribulation will bring you closer to Me than you ever thought possible.

CHAPTER 11

THE DAWNING

F irst Fruits 16th Nissan 5775; April 5th 2015.

Yeshua Speaks: Soon it will be the dawning of the Day of Adonai; it will be just like any other day and yet it will be unlike any other day. There have been and are many warnings and harbingers that herald the approach of this day. The times that you are living in are clearly foretold in the Scriptures and I Myself outlined them in detail to My disciples. My words are not limited by time. They believed that the days that they lived in were so wicked and murderous that surely, with the destruction of the temple in the Holy City, I was just around the corner. The words I spoke were fresh in their spirits and minds and they lived in the wonderful expectation that I would soon be reunited with them.

They were looking for the dawning of the day when I would return. They would actually look to the heavens, remembering My words: *Luke 21:25-28 "There will appear signs in the sun, moon and stars; and on earth, nations will be in anxiety and bewilderment at the sound and surge of the sea, as people faint with fear at the prospect of what is overtaking the world; for the powers in heaven will be shaken. And then they will see the Son of Man coming in a cloud with tremendous power and glory. When these things start to happen, stand up and hold your heads high; because you are about to be liberated!" CJB.*

Each day there lived in their hearts the wonderful expectation and the lingering thought: *"Will it be today?" "Will this be the day of His appearing?"* The disciples longed for the dawning of that day. They mused*:*

"How my heart aches and longs for Him."

"How I long for those times when He spoke to me, when He looked lovingly into my eyes, so close to me that I could reach out and touch Him."

"I didn't understand the depth and fullness of His words, but they burn within my heart each and every day."

"How I long for Him."

"I remember His words to me and I will never forget them, but nonetheless at the dawning of each day, I will look for Him, and when that day is done I will look again to the dawning of the next new day."

"This is how I live my life."

"This is my focus."

"Will this be the day of His return?"

This is how you are to live and survive in these last days. I am the only reality in your life; I am your anchor in the storms; I am the one true foundation; for the world you are living in is an illusion propped up by nefarious schemes of money-laundering and all manner of wickedness that drives your western societies. You have blinders on your eyes led along the path of "this is the way it has always been and nothing bad will ever happen to us and our way of life." It is time to wake up from your slumber; the Day of Adonai is approaching and you need to be ready like the ten bridesmaids; having your lamps ready so that you can come into the wedding feast of the Lamb.

Remember well the story that although there were ten ready and waiting, five of them were not fully prepared. Their heart attitude was right, but they had not taken the time to fully prepare themselves and they found themselves locked out. You need to ensure that your lamps are ready and that you have a full supply of My Ruach HaKodesh oil when I appear. *** Matthew 25:1-13 CJB.

Look to your heart; for by My Spirit I am alive within you. When I am approaching My Spirit will burn within you. You don't need a news broadcast to tell you I am coming; you will know. Many are looking for signs of My appearing and they are indeed present and obvious, but be careful and be warned that you need to be looking for Me in your heart and not out there somewhere.

My people were looking for a sign and even though I was standing in their very midst performing miracles, they rejected the plain clear physical evidence that I was their Messiah. Why could they not see? Mainly because I was not what they were expecting! They were looking for a king who would endorse their lifestyles; promote the religious leaders to still higher positions; give them slaves to cater for their every whim; subdue all of their enemies particularly the Roman Empire; put them in charge and prosper and bless not only them but the whole nation of Israel and all that was foreshadowed in the Scriptures. Their god - their way.

I was a great disappointment to them and their lofty goals and ambitions:

"But this Yeshua is from Nazareth and nothing good has ever come out of that town. It's not even on our radar."

"If this man is the Messiah, we would know because it's our job, that's who we are."

"We are the religious leaders and when he comes we will be the first to know."

"By his own words, he is guilty of blasphemy and must be put to death!"

Mark 14:61-64 ....Again the cohen hagadol questioned him: "Are you the Mashiach, Ben-HaM'vorakh?"

"I AM," answered Yeshua. "Moreover, you will see the Son of Man sitting at the right hand of HaG'vurah and coming on the clouds of heaven."

At this, the cohen hagadol tore his clothes and said, "Why do we still need witnesses? You heard him blaspheme! What is your decision?" And they all declared him guilty and subject to the death penalty. CJB.

Matthew 26:63-66 Yeshua remained silent. The cohen hagadol said to him, "I put you under oath! By the living God, tell us if you are the Mashiach, the Son of God!"

Yeshua said to him, "The words are your own. But I tell you that one day you will see the Son of Man sitting at the right hand of HaG'vurah and coming on the clouds of heaven."

At this, the cohen hagadol tore his robes. "Blasphemy!" he said. "Why do we still need witnesses? You heard him blaspheme! What is your verdict?" "Guilty," they answered. "He deserves death!" CJB.

And so, it will be when I come again, but this time I will be coming as the King of kings and Lord of lords and will no longer be subjected to the power of the adversary, and his cronies. All will be swept away by My incoming army of holy angels. It will not be as your religious leaders of today are telling you. I will not fit into any of their religious boxes any more than I did the religious boxes of the religious leaders of old. It will not be as you think or imagine or dream or wish.

Ehyeh Asher Ehyeh - I Am who I Am and will Be who I will Be, nothing held back any more. I will no longer conform to your understanding of Me, I will be the Alev Tav that is spoken of so clearly in the Scriptures:

Revelation 21:5-6 Then the One sitting on the throne said, "Look! I am making everything new!"

Also he said, "Write, 'These words are true and trustworthy!'" And he said to me, "It is done! I am the 'A' and the 'Z,' the Beginning and the End. To anyone who is thirsty I myself will give water free of charge from the Fountain of Life." CJB.

I have always been, I always am and I always will be. The dawning of My appearing grows closer every day. You cannot even begin to imagine what that means. Brighter than the sun is My glorious appearance. It will blind you, it will strike you down and it is only as I touch you that you will be able to rise again. But you will no longer be the same, for you will rise to stand and walk in My World, My Kingdom. The old will be done away with —"Look! I am making everything new!" and that means you through and through; transformed to live in My presence forever; united in Me no longer looking for the dawning of the Day of the Lord; because you will be walking with Me on this your first day in the Kingdom of Heaven.

Revelation 21:5 Then the One sitting on the throne said, "Look! I am making everything new!" Also he said, "Write, 'These words are true and trustworthy!'" CJB.

Words cannot express the glorious transformation that awaits you all as you cross over into the eternal Kingdom. I am your King and in the days that are left to you on this earth let go of all of your preconceived ideas of what My Kingdom will look like. Know that it is far greater and more magnificent and more glorious and more colourful and more fragrant beyond your wildest imagination. Prepare your hearts for the just and righteous King that I am and do all to please Me and Me only in these days.

Who is your current king? Whose orders do you obey? This is a question for you to answer. Most of you serve and worship yourselves and you have made yourselves king of your own lives, seeking only to fulfil your own desires. This is a matter for you to allow My Ruach HaKodesh to examine your life, your loves, your motives, your attitudes, your inner private self in the light of My coming Kingdom. It is time for you to do the King's bidding and begin to prepare your hearts and thinking so that you are Kingly minded; remembering that there is now a King in your life who will be served as the King of kings in His Kingdom.

The Dawning Is Nigh: There has been grace and mercy extended to you in your life to lead you into being a citizen of the coming Kingdom; Ruach HaKodesh is leading, teaching and training you day by day to prepare your spirit for the coming of the King. Begin this very day to honour and worship Yahweh and Yeshua. Enjoy the intimacy of Ruach HaKodesh that brings you into the presence of the King whose heart and desire is to fellowship and commune with you forever.

Yeshua is not a King afar off; He is intimate and personal but is also your King. This is difficult for you to grasp that someone so exalted can be at the same time so humble; embracing every member of the community of Heaven with tenderness and love, yet powerful and glorious beyond words. This is Yahweh; His nature is a mystery. So powerful yet so gentle, so righteous and just but yet so forgiving. Glorious, Holy, Majestic, no beginning, no ending. "*Ehyeh Asher Ehyeh* - I Am who I Am and will Be who I will Be; nothing held back any more; He wants us along for the eternal ride to enjoy all that He is - from eternity past to eternity future.

Yahweh's King of Righteousness and our Great Cohen Hagadol, Yeshua His Son, is coming soon to set up this Kingdom. It is the midnight hour and the dawning of the day of Messiah Yeshua, the King of kings is at hand.

*Hebrews 7:17-21 It is stated***,** *"You are a cohen FOREVER, to be compared with Malki-Tzedek."*

Thus, on the one hand, the earlier rule is set aside because of its weakness and inefficacy (for the Torah did not bring anything to the goal); and, on the other hand, a hope of something better is introduced, through which we are drawing near to God.

What is more, God swore an oath. For no oath was sworn in connection with those who become cohanim now; but Yeshua became a cohen by the oath which God swore when he said to him, "Adonai has sworn and will not change his mind, 'You are a cohen forever.'" CJB.

The Dawning was first published in G.I.F.T Godly Insights For Today eBook Season Eight in 2015. The Dawning is included in Season Nine Troubled Waters Dead Ahead eBook and Paperback.

***Matthew 25:1-13 "The Kingdom of Heaven at that time will be like ten bridesmaids who took their lamps and went out to meet the groom. Five of them were foolish and five were sensible. The foolish ones took lamps with them but no oil, whereas the others took flasks of oil with their lamps.

Now the bridegroom was late, so they all went to sleep. It was the middle of the night when the cry rang out, 'The bridegroom is here! Go out to meet him!' The girls all woke up and prepared their lamps for lighting. The foolish ones said to the sensible ones, 'Give us some of your oil, because our lamps are going out.' 'No,' they replied, 'there may not be enough for both you and us. Go to the oil dealers and buy some for yourselves.'

But as they were going off to buy, the bridegroom came. Those who were ready went with him to the wedding feast, and the door was shut. Later, the other bridesmaids came. 'Sir! Sir!' they cried, 'Let us in!' But he answered, 'Indeed! I tell you, I don't know you!' So stay alert, because you know neither the day nor the hour. CJB.

CHAPTER 12
CONSTANCY

March 31st 2015; 11th Nisan 5775.

Definition: steadfastness, as in purpose or affection; faithfulness. The condition or quality of being constant; changelessness.

Ruach HaKodesh Speaks: Yeshua the Messiah is the same yesterday, today and forever. *Hebrews 13:8 Yeshua the Messiah is the same yesterday, today and forever. CJB*. Yeshua is your sure foundation; the rock upon which your relationship with Yahweh is secured. He is Yahweh's salvation and "there is no other name under Heaven given to mankind by whom we must be saved!" *Acts 4:11-12 "This Yeshua is the stone rejected by you builders which has become the cornerstone. There is salvation in no one else! For there is no other name under heaven given to mankind by whom we must be saved!" CJB*.

He redeemed you from your sinful state by His own bloody sacrificial death from the power of sin over your lives. The sweet fellowship that Adam and Eve had with the Creator of all things was again made possible; the New

Covenant relationship forged in His blood broke the curse of separation that began in the Garden of Eden.

Yeshua is Himself God; there can be no surer guarantee that your trust in Him as Yahweh's Redeemer is a trust well founded. *John 1:1 In the beginning was the Word, and the Word was with God, and the Word was God. CJB.*

Yahweh installed Yeshua by an oath as a Priest of the order of Malki-Tzedek forever. *Hebrews 7:21 but Yeshua became a cohen by the oath which God swore when he said to him, "Adonai has sworn and will not change his mind, 'You are a cohen forever.'" CJB.*

Psalm 110:4 Adonai has sworn it, and he will never retract - "You are a cohen forever, to be compared with Malki-Tzedek." CJB.

Yeshua is the great eternal high priest now sitting at the right hand of Yahweh outside of your timeframe, who forever was, forever is and forever will be. Yahweh entered into covenant relationship with Abraham and by the physical act of circumcision the covenant was entered into that day laying the foundation for the salvation of all of mankind. It was to Abraham's seed that Yahweh promised salvation. Yeshua became that seed as the Son of Man when He came to earth and was the instrument in Yahweh's hands that reversed the curse of bondage to Satan, the king of the earth.

Yeshua was in God's plan for the redemption of mankind from the very beginning; it succeeded so powerfully and beautifully because Yeshua's Constancy and permanence from the beginning of time and even before. He is central to Yahweh's unfolding great love. The execution stake stands at the crossroads where eternity past meets eternity future. *Psalm 41:14 (13) Blessed be Adonai the*

God of Isra'el from eternity past to eternity future. Amen. Amen. CJB.

He is before all, in all and after all. There was nothing that came into existence that did not have His indelible mark upon it. *John 1:3 All things came to be through him, and without him nothing made had being. CJB.* He is the one who literally holds all things together right down to the sub atomic particles that are foundational to everything you touch, handle, see and experience with your physical bodies.

Colossians 1:17 He existed before all things, and he holds everything together CJB; You were dead under the penalty of your disobedience of Yahweh's Torah. It was violated the moment that you were born because you were bound by the power of sin and the death curse it put you under.

Yeshua conquered death and is the firstborn of the subjects of Yahweh's new Kingdom. He was promoted to the right hand of Abba to sit and fellowship with Him forever because of His obedient servitude as the Lamb of God that took away the sin of the world. He will return to judge and destroy the enemies of Abba. He is the one to whom Abba has entrusted all judgments; not only the inhabitants of the earth; but of Satan himself, his kingdom of Death and Hades; and all of the fallen angels and hosts of darkness that have aligned themselves with him.

Psalm 110 Yahweh says to my Lord, "Sit at my right hand, until I make your enemies your footstool for your feet."

Yahweh will send out the rod of your strength out of Zion. Rule among your enemies

Your people offer themselves willingly in the day of your power, in holy array. Out of the womb of the morning, you have the dew of your youth.

Yahweh has sworn, and will not change his mind: "You are a priest forever in the order of Melchizedek."

The Lord is at your right hand. He will crush kings in the day of his wrath.

He will judge among the nations. He will heap up dead bodies. He will crush the ruler of the whole earth.

He will drink of the brook on the way; therefore he will lift up his head. WEB.

Yeshua Is Constancy!

He is the Word of God settled forever in Heaven: *John 1:1 In the beginning was the Word, and the Word was with God, and the Word was God. CJB.*

He is the Mediator or Daysman of Heaven: *Daysman definition; An adjudicator, judge, or intermediary.*

1 Timothy 2:5 For there is one God and one mediator between God and men, the man Christ Jesus; WEB.

Job 9:32-33 For he is not a man, as I am, that I should answer him, and we should come together in judgment. Neither is there any daysman betwixt us, that might lay his hand upon us both. KJV.

The Overseer of all of Abba's Kingdom: *Luke 4:43 But he said to them, "I must announce the Good News of the Kingdom of God to the other towns too — this is why I was sent." CJB.*

Luke 11:20 But if I drive out demons by the finger of God, then the Kingdom of God has come upon you! CJB.

Luke 17:21 "nor will people be able to say, 'Look! Here it is!' or, 'Over there!' Because, you see, the Kingdom of God is among you." CJB.

Matthew 28:18 Yeshua came and talked with them. He said, "All authority in heaven and on earth has been given to me." CJB.

The Prince of Peace: *Isaiah 9:6 For a child is born to us. A* son is given to us; and the government will be on his shoulders. His name will be called Wonderful Counselor, Mighty God, Everlasting Father, Prince of Peace. WEB.

The King of Kings: *1 Timothy 6:14-16 that you keep the commandment without spot, blameless until the appearing of our Lord Jesus Christ, which at the right time he will show, who is the blessed and only Ruler, the King of kings and Lord of lords. He alone has immortality, dwelling in unapproachable light, whom no man has seen nor can see, to whom be honor and eternal power. Amen. WEB.*

The King of Righteousness: *Hebrews 7:2 also Avraham gave him a tenth of everything. Now first of all, by translation of his name, he is "king of righteousness"; and then he is also king of Shalem, which means "king of peace." CJB.*

He is Unchangeable: *Hebrews 6:17 Therefore, when God wanted to demonstrate still more convincingly the unchangeable character of his intentions to those who were to receive what he had promised, he added an oath to the promise; CJB.*

He is Faithful: *Romans 3:22 and it is a righteousness that comes from God, through the faithfulness of Yeshua the Messiah, to all who continue trusting. For it makes no difference whether one is a Jew or a Gentile; CJB.*

He is Our Advocate - Loyal: *1 John 2:1-3 My little children, these things write I unto you, that ye sin not. And if any man sin, we have an advocate with the Father, Jesus Christ the righteous: And he is the propitiation for our sins: and not for ours only, but also for the sins of the whole world. And hereby we do know that we know him, if we keep his commandments. KJV.*

He is Stable: *Hebrews 13:8 Yeshua the Messiah is the same yesterday, today and forever. CJB.*

He is Totally Trustworthy: *Hebrews 10:23 Let us continue holding fast to the hope we acknowledge, without* *wavering; for the One who made the promise is trustworthy. CJB.*

He is Truth: *John 1:17 For the Torah was given through Moshe; grace and truth came through Yeshua the Messiah. CJB.*

John 14:6 Yeshua said, "I AM the Way — and the Truth and the Life; no one comes to the Father except through me. CJB.

He is Love: *Romans 8:35 Who will separate us from the love of the Messiah? Trouble? Hardship? Persecution? Hunger? Poverty? Danger? War? CJB.*

Romans 8:39 neither powers above nor powers below, nor any other created thing will be able to separate us from the love of God which comes to us through the Messiah Yeshua, our Lord. CJB.

He is Full of Abba's Glory: *Matthew 16:27 For the Son of Man will come in the glory of his Father with his angels, and then he will render to everyone according to his deeds. WEB.*

Mark 8:38 For whoever will be ashamed of me and of my words in this adulterous and sinful generation, the Son of Man also will be ashamed of him when he comes in his Father's glory with the holy angels." WEB.

He is Holy: *Luke 1:35 The angel answered her, "The Ruach HaKodesh will come over you, the power of Ha'Elyon will cover you. Therefore the holy child born to you will be called the Son of God. CJB.*

John 6:69 We have trusted, and we know that you are the Holy One of God." CJB.

Mark 1:24 "What do you want with us, Yeshua from Natzeret? Have you come to destroy us? I know who you are — the Holy One of God!" CJB.

He is Righteous: *Philippians 1:11 filled with the fruit of righteousness that comes through Yeshua the Messiah — to the glory and praise of God. CJB.*

Philippians 3:9 and be found in union with him, not having any righteousness of my own based on legalism, but having that righteousness which comes through the Messiah's faithfulness, the righteousness from God based on trust. CJB.

He is Mighty: *Luke 1:69 by raising up for us a mighty Deliverer who is a descendant of his servant David. CJB.*

Ephesians 6:10 Finally, grow powerful in union with the Lord, in union with his mighty strength! CJB.

He is Zealous: *John 2:17 (His talmidim later recalled that the Tanakh says, "Zeal for your house will devour me.") CJB.*

Philippians 1:6 And I am sure of this: that the One who began a good work among you will keep it growing until it is completed on the Day of the Messiah Yeshua. CJB.

He is Firm and Faithful: *Revelation 3:14 "To the angel of the assembly in Laodicea write: "The Amen, the Faithful and True Witness, the Beginning of God's creation, says these things: WEB.*

He Is Constancy!

CHAPTER 13

RETRIBUTION

March 31st 2015; 11th Nisan 5775.

Definition: recompense, reward. The dispensing or receiving of reward or punishment especially in the hereafter.

Yahweh Speaks: I am the God of retribution and I will judge the works of man with My strong hand of vengeance. It will be enacted upon all who have willingly and deliberately violated My holy righteous laws; who have sought to destroy My people and all who are by faith in My Son Yeshua; My family. They have aligned themselves with Satan the adversary; who has shared the riches of his earthly kingdom with them promising them a share in all the stolen riches plundered by murder, rape, pillage and the mutilation of individuals, tribes and nations.

He promised them a share in his kingdom if they would sell their souls to him. He discounted Me and My righteous ones as so much trash and railed at us as being insignificant. Those that are sold out to him fail to see a very obvious problem when dealing with this treacherous being;

he never had any intention of keeping his end of the bargain or contract with them.

Whenever it suits his purposes he can and has repeatedly destroyed them; sneering at their allegiance to him and any achievements made for the cause. He laughs mockingly as his servants are slaughtered before his very eyes and delights to see their blood poured out in servitude to him. They have all responded to his great deception "I will give you all the kingdoms of the world, and their glory, if you will fall down and worship me."

My Son Yeshua was tempted in this very way. The fatal flaw for humans is that they are human and Satan knows that he would never be held to account for any of his promises; firstly he is the father of lies and secondly without so much as a second thought he could annihilate anyone who became any sort of threat. Being under his authority and control all he had to do was wait until they died or kill them if they no longer suited his vile and evil purposes.

Luke 4:5-7 The devil, leading him up on a high mountain, showed him all the kingdoms of the world in a moment of time. The devil said to him, "I will give you all this authority, and their glory, for it has been delivered to me; and I give it to whomever I want. If you therefore will worship before me, it will all be yours." WEB.

He rules his kingdom by a litany of lies, stealth and deception because evil men's hearts are so full of greed and corruption. The elite of this world as they call themselves; are the prime targets for him to use to achieve his purposes. They have sold out to him and are willing to die for him and together with millions of others are growing into an army that is being prepared for the great end time battles.

THOMAS A PETTERSON

He is the tyrant of all tyrants and is by all means preparing a vicious, hateful army that delights in the slaughter of innocents, babies, children, men and women, even tearing them apart and eating their flesh. Their hearts are full of bloodlust; the more they kill, the more they have to kill to satisfy their cravings for rape, murder, beheadings, torture, mutilation; all reflecting the nature of their king and master whose nature and actions are now becoming their way of life.

He is on a mission to destroy not only the Jews and all of My righteous ones but all of mankind; he knows that I am a holy righteous God who forgives and can change the hearts of his slaves who have turned their back on him and become traitors to his cause. When they die in battle for Me they will look heavenwards to Me and like Stephen and My Son Yeshua pray "Abba forgive them for they know not what they are doing."

Luke 23:34 Jesus said, "Father, forgive them, for they don't know what they are doing." Dividing his garments among them, they cast lots. WEB.

My children have a clear understanding that others like them are slaves to sin and that they are under the devil's power of control operating in their lives; causing them to be caught up in all manner of wickedness. In asking Me to forgive them they are freeing themselves from their own unforgiveness towards the people and events involved; releasing them into My hands so that they will have a further opportunity of confession and repentance to change their allegiance from the kingdom of darkness to the Kingdom of glorious light. The matter of revenge and justice is thus put back in My hands where it rightly belongs.

Romans 12:19-21 Don't seek revenge yourselves, beloved, but give place to God's wrath. For it is written, "Vengeance belongs to me; I will repay, says the Lord."

Therefore "If your enemy is hungry, feed him. If he is thirsty, give him a drink. For in doing so, you will heap coals of fire on his head." Don't be overcome by evil, but overcome evil with good. WEB.

Yeshua Speaks: Remember Paul was a persecutor of the followers of The Way. He persecuted the disciples and all who followed their teachings and had allegiance to Yeshua their Messiah. What a hopeless case.... "and the witnesses laid down their coats at the feet of a young man named Sha'ul." There stood Stephen; as he was being stoned to death he prayed "Lord Yeshua! Receive my spirit!" Then he knelt down and shouted out, "Lord! Don't hold this sin against them!" With that, he died.

Acts 7:58b-60 .....And the witnesses laid down their coats at the feet of a young man named Sha'ul.

As they were stoning him, Stephen called out to God, "Lord Yeshua! Receive my spirit!" Then he kneeled down and shouted out, "Lord! Don't hold this sin against them!" With that, he died. CJB.

Paul was one that I forgave and after meeting him on the road to Damascus. I turned his misdirected allegiance into a 'faithful unto death' disciple who affected the whole family of God in his ministry and writings.

Acts 9:3-6 He was on the road and nearing Dammesek, when suddenly a light from heaven flashed all around him.

Falling to the ground, he heard a voice saying to him, "Sha'ul! Sha'ul! Why do you keep persecuting me?"

"Sir, who are you?" he asked. "I am Yeshua, and you are persecuting me. But get up, and go into the city, and you will be told what you have to do." CJB.

Yahweh Speaks: It is not up to you to seek revenge on

those that have harmed you and are even now killing Christians all across the globe. Vengeance is mine I will repay, thus says the Lord. *Romans 12:19 Never seek revenge, my friends; instead, leave that to God's anger; for in the Tanakh it is written, "Adonai says, 'Vengeance is my responsibility; I will repay.'" CJB.*

My day of retribution is fast approaching; always remember that wickedness cannot be overcome by killing people because on a moment's reflection it would never end. Your humanity will cause you to embark on a course of 'fix it actions' that in the end will fail and ultimately only prolong Satan's reign of your world. My restorative retribution also speaks of rewards and not just punishment and separation. I am a merciful Elohim full of glory and grace and My righteous judgments will fall on every human, every angel, and every spirit from the smallest to the greatest. None will escape.

My retribution will be thorough beyond your understanding of what thorough means. My Son Yeshua will cause all to stand before Him and My righteous judgments will be executed by Him and none will escape; nothing will remain hidden, every idle word, every sin, every thought, every action will be exposed to My glorious light. None will escape, none will be overlooked. *Ecclesiastes 12:14 For God will bring every work into judgment, with every hidden thing, whether it is good, or whether it is evil. WEB.*

In the days that lay ahead look not to watch evil and wicked things others are doing; continually look to your own heart, examine your own thoughts, words, actions and motives; confessing your sins and shortcomings at every opportunity; being careful to remain tuned into Ruach HaKodesh in these most uncertain times. *Matthew 12:36*

Moreover, I tell you this: on the Day of Judgment people will have to give account for every careless word they have spoken; CJB.

My justice is not like your justice which often times is very shallow; you are limited by time and it is flavoured by your own life experience and your own values. Yours is not a comprehensive justice and you are naïve to think that I will carry out My judgments based only on what is happening in the world today. These end times are the culmination of treachery, wickedness, evil, betrayal, murder beyond your comprehension. You have little understanding of the centuries of evil and wickedness that have and are still operating in high places.

Retribution is My prerogative. I am the only one who can justly repay each and every one based not only on your limited understanding and values you have gained in your short time on the earth; but in the light of eternity past, the present and all the way into eternity future. You must allow Me to carry out vengeance My way and in My time.

You will soon be going through tough times of tribulation as the evil one steps up his program to destroy you and My Holy nation and all who have put their trust in My Son Yeshua. Do all that you can do that is honourable and just and true to your own values; forgive those that seek to harm you; the moment that you do they will become My problem and I will intervene on your behalf and protect, lead and guide you as I have promised. I am true to My word and in these trying times you can depend on Me. I have stayed My hand of vengeance; it is so powerful and swift that when released it will bring a total and complete end to the kingdom of darkness on the earth. Satan will be totally defeated and all who have allegiance to him will be annihilated by the sword of fire coming forth from the mouth of My Son Yeshua.

Revelation 19:11-21 "Next I saw heaven opened, and there before me was a white horse. Sitting on it was the one called Faithful and True, and it is in righteousness that he passes judgment and goes to battle.

His eyes were like a fiery flame, and on his head were many royal crowns. And he had a name written which no one knew but himself. He was wearing a robe that had been soaked in blood, and the name by which he is called is, "THE WORD OF GOD."

The armies of heaven, clothed in fine linen, white and pure, were following him on white horses. And out of his mouth comes a sharp sword with which to strike down nations — "He will rule them with a staff of iron." It is he who treads the winepress from which flows the wine of the furious rage of Adonai, God of heaven's armies. And on his robe and on his thigh he has a name written: "KING OF KINGS AND LORD OF LORDS

Then I saw an angel standing in the sun, and he cried out in a loud voice to all the birds that fly about in mid-heaven, "Come, gather together for the great feast God is giving, to eat the flesh of kings, the flesh of generals, the flesh of important men, the flesh of horses and their riders and the flesh of all kinds of people, free and slave, small and great!"

I saw the beast and the kings of the earth and their armies gathered together to do battle with the rider of the horse and his army. But the beast was taken captive, and with it the false prophet who, in its presence, had done the miracles which he had used to deceive those who had received the mark of the beast and those who had worshipped his image. The beast and the false prophet were both thrown alive into the lake of fire that burns with sulfur.

The rest were killed with the sword that goes out of the

mouth of the rider on the horse, and all the birds gorged them-
selves on their flesh. CJB.

Nothing that is happening is out of My control; I can stop it immediately if I so choose. Never doubt that; know that there is a multitude of evil and wickedness that is being dealt with; not just the issues that you have experienced in your lifetime and your recorded history.

My retribution will be thorough and complete judging all matters from before the beginning of time; together with issues that occurred both inside and outside of time which you have no knowledge of. I will judge ALL the hidden things. My judgments will be swift, total and complete and it will take an eternity for you to understand My great love, My great justice, My great mercy, My great patience, My holy anger.

You are now entering into the time of My retribution. I do all things well; as I always have and always will. I am always in control as I have always been and always will be. Vengeance is always My prerogative; but even in pouring out My vengeance it will be just and measured. Retribution is not a popular word; but I am the God of retribution and it is a necessary part of My nature to bring you all into a holy righteous state so that we can fellowship together forever.

Kingdoms on your earth have come and gone but My Kingdom and the Kingdom of My Son will stand forever; for it is not founded on wrong foundations. Yeshua My Son is the foundation, the stone rejected by the builders that has now become the very cornerstone of My Kingdom. *Ephesians 2:19-22 So then, you are no longer foreigners and strangers. On the contrary, you are fellow- citizens with God's people and members of God's family. You have been built on the foundation of the emissaries and the prophets, with the corner-stone being Yeshua the Messiah himself.*

In union with him the whole building is held together, and it is growing into a holy temple in union with the Lord. Yes, in union with him, you yourselves are being built together into a spiritual dwelling- place for God! CJB.

My truth, My justice, My Righteousness, My holiness, My glory are the foundation stones upon which My marvellous eternal Kingdom will stand. You see in a mirror dimly whilst ever you are on earth; when you are transformed I will remove the scales from your eyes so that you will begin to see and understand and experience all that I am. *1 Corinthians 13:12 For now [in this time of imperfection] we see in a mirror dimly [a blurred reflection, a riddle, an enigma], but then [when the time of perfection comes we will see reality] face to face. Now I know in part [just in fragments], but then I will know fully, just as I have been fully known [by God]. AMP.*

I am the eternal one that existed before the beginning of time. I plan to share the great coming Kingdom with all who accept and have put their trust in My Son; who is your salvation and My plan of redemption for you all.

Break off the remaining shackles of the evil one and let your one desire be to sit in My presence and learn more of My ways. The early disciples committed themselves to the word and prayer. Having been baptised in the Ruach HaKodesh and given their heavenly language they used this gift as a foundation for the messianic believers and all who were to follow. My Son Yeshua always found the time to be by Himself so that He could communicate with Me.

It is fitting that all modern-day disciples should also commit themselves to the study of the Word and prayer and set aside time each day to communicate with Heaven; as did the apostles in the book of Acts.

Acts 6:4 But we will continue steadfastly in prayer and in the ministry of the word." WEB.

This will enable Me to wrap up all of My dealings and interaction with My creation; and assist the hosts of Heaven in bringing the adversary before the courts of Heaven so that My just and righteous judgment can fall on him and all of the hosts of darkness.

The hour of My Retribution is upon you.

EPILOGUE

The Aaronic Blessing:
Numbers 6:24-26. CJB.

'Y'VAREKH'KHA ADONAI V'YISHMEREKHA.
May *Adonai* bless you
and keep you.

YA'ER ADONAI PANAV ELEIKHA VICHUNEKKA.
May *Adonai* make his face shine on you
and show you his favor.

YISSA ADONAI PANAV ELEIKHA V'YASEM L'KHA SHALOM.
May *Adonai* lift up his face toward you
and give you peace.

≈

AFTERWORD

I trust that these words will identify what you need to do to prepare yourselves as your faith and trust in Yeshua, Yahweh and the leading of Ruach HaKodesh will come under intense attack in the not too distant future.

The harbinger of Anti-Semitism is now front-page news and rising in ferocity and frequency. Today it is the Jews, tomorrow it will be you and all who have put their faith and trust in Yahweh, the God of Israel. It will be a **Calamity** for all. Be assured of His **Constancy**, His unfailing love, and His **Righteousness,** and address your **Caveat** of unbelief and be much in prayer and study of His Word to give you the **Fortitude** you'll need to face your season of **Tribulation** that none will escape.

Through this process He will refine you in the furnace of affliction; refine you and commission you giving you your **New Shoes**. He will provide for you often through the generosity of others who are called to share His **Blessing Sandwiches**. Receive them with a humble grateful heart and always share them with others. You will not only survive but thrive.

Prepare your heart, mind and spirit as led by Ruach HaKodesh. Explore your relationship with Yeshua **The Greatest Gift** and let it become your daily focus falling more in love with the lover of your soul; your Saviour, Redeemer and soon coming King. Allow Ruach HaKodesh to become your paraclete and ever-present faithful companion to lead and guide you in all your ways each and every day.

Pray for a fresh infilling of Ruach HaKodesh every day and keep short accounts dealing with unconfessed sin as by nature it is ever crouching at your door. Stick to Yeshua like glue and tune your spiritual radio to the broadcasts of heaven. Stay tuned in being careful not to go off station.

It will soon be **The Dawning** of the Lord's Day our great and wonderful hope of a forever future with Yeshua, Yahweh, Ruach HaKodesh, millions of angels and departed saints.

A brand-new world and Kingdom that is beyond the ability of human words to describe.

Yahweh is Holy and Righteous and all the works of man both good and evil will come before Him because He is the God of **Retribution.** We as humans are not comfortable with things we cannot understand or fathom. Yahweh's ways are past finding out and cannot be understood through the lens of our humanity. *Isaiah 55:8-9 "For my thoughts are not your thoughts, and your ways are not my ways," says Yahweh. For as the heavens are higher than the earth, so are my ways higher than your ways, and my thoughts than your thoughts." WEB.*

Retribution gives some insight into Yahweh's greater wisdom; but although we cannot think like Yahweh we can absolutely trust Him and be the beneficiaries of His Great Love, His Infinite Wisdom and His Just and Righteous

Rulings. A God that spared not His very own Son from a bloody sacrificial death to save us from being eternally separated from Him and His future Kingdom that He has already prepared for all who will believe in Him and His Son.

Isaiah 55:1 "Hey! Come, everyone who thirsts, to the waters! Come, he who has no money, buy, and eat! Yes, come, buy wine and milk without money and without price. WEB.

Yahweh Loves You with a Great Love that is past finding out or understanding. He sent fresh bread from heaven His Son Yeshua that all who eat of Him will live forever. Yeshua testified in John 6:51:

"I am the living bread which came down out of heaven. If anyone eats of this bread, he will live forever. Yes, the bread which I will give for the life of the world is my flesh." WEB.

May He give you the courage to face and deal with any issues in your life that these words prompt you with the help of Ruach HaKodesh to address.

Thomas A Petterson
Prophetic Scribe

End Note:

The Shaking and Awakening has 13 chapters which are highlighted above.

The number 13 in Hebrew is echad = One. *Deuteronomy 6:4 "Sh'ma, Yisra'el! Adonai Eloheinu, Adonai echad [Hear, Isra'el! Adonai our God, Adonai is one]; CJB.*

Mark 12:29 Yeshua answered, "The most important is, 'Sh'ma Yisra'el, Adonai Eloheinu, Adonai echad [Hear, O Isra'el, the Lord our God, the Lord is one] CJB.

ABOUT THE AUTHOR

Thomas Petterson comes from a family with a rich Christian heritage. His Great Grandfather, Colonel Sharpe, was known as the Fiery Prophet in the Salvation Army. Thomas was raised in the Salvation Army; at age seven his family moved to the Pymble Baptist Church where he spent most of his teenage years.

At age sixteen he was drawn to the bedside of his recently departed grandmother, knelt down and gave his life to Jesus. Many years later he discovered that his grandmother had been praying for her grandsons to be saved and filled with the Holy Spirit.

Thomas spent the next decade searching for a deeper relationship with God. He was baptised in the Holy Spirit at a Holy Spirit Teaching Seminar in Sydney in 1976 where his life took on a whole new dimension. He married his sweetheart Julie-Ann in 1977 and joined by God as a team; they have been following Him wherever He has directed them.

In 1981 he left the family business and Thomas began the journey of discovering who he was in Jesus Christ. Together, with his wife Julie-Ann, they bought a motel in Nowra; it was in the office of the complex one morning as he was meditating, praying and looking at the Nowra bridge across the river he started to write down what he heard the Holy Spirit say……. "Just as the bridge you are looking at is 100 years old"….Thomas thought that's ridiculous, screwed up the paper and threw it in the bin.

The next day the local paper ran a front-page article on how the bridge was 100 years old and had been re-opened after renovations. He realised that he really had heard from the Lord and needed to start taking notice of what the Holy Spirit was telling him.

G.I.F.T Godly Insights For Today is a result of over 40 years of listening to the Holy Spirit.

During the late 60s & 70s, Thomas was the technical director for Young World Singers who conducted evangelistic outreach concerts across Australia, New Zealand, South East Asia and Papua New Guinea.

He attended Vision Christian College and holds a Certificate in Biblical Studies with honours 1998; Associate Diploma in Biblical Studies with Honours 1998; Diploma in Ministry with honours 1999 and Diploma in Theology with Honours 2001.

Together with his wife ran a Christian Convention Centre in Nowra and established and ran a Christian Parent Controlled School on the NSW South Coast.

They became qualified prayer counsellors through VMTC Victorious Ministries Through Christ in 1986 and volunteered as counsellors for 5 years. Music has been a big part of their lives, running music groups, concerts, Christian art exhibitions and prayer fellowships.

A family trip to Israel in 1989 added another dimension to his spiritual life and sent him on a fresh journey to discover the Hebrew roots of his Christian faith.

Thomas has been married to Julie-Ann for over 45 years and they now reside in Canberra, Australia.

Also by Thomas A Petterson

G.I.F.T Season Nine:

Troubled Waters Dead Ahead

The World is now entering Troubled Waters as the master of evil is inspiring his legions of fallen angels to commit unthinkable atrocities around the globe.

Don't let attacks, whether they be physical, emotional or spiritual, deter you from becoming the real you, united with the Father through Yeshua, led and directed by the Holy Spirit each and every day, every step of the way, led and fed supernaturally through these trying and testing times.

www.ingramcontent.com/pod-product-compliance
Lightning Source LLC
Chambersburg PA
CBHW021935040426
42448CB00008B/1082